BAKE IT TILL YOU MAKE IT

BAKE IT TILL YOU MAKE IT

Breaking Bread, Building Resilience

The First Of Its Kind Mental Health & Resilience Cookbook

By Dayna Altman

Dear Human,

Take a moment and think about the last time you felt represented in the media. Whether it be on a tv show or in a book or magazine, when did you look and say, "oh..they get me!" Or "they look like me" or even, "they live like me!"

If you are like most adults in America, you consume about 11 hours of media content per day. While much of our initial searches or interests may be sparked for entertainment purposes only, at some point during the viewing process or otherwise (through ads, commercials or articles), consumers report feeling disappointed as a result of feeling under-represented (if represented at all).

I have seen this disconnect between our daily lives and the lives we see or hear about since I was a little girl. This dates back to kindergarten playing with Barbie Dolls who did not have my curly hair, skin tone coloring or a career in entrepreneurship. And while this all may be a bit of an unfair burden to place solely on Barbie, I knew when I embarked on creating the first of its kind mental health and resilience cookbook, I needed to include all stories. I wanted to create a place where people felt seen and heard, whether it was directly by contributing to the book or by being the consumer and hopefully: connecting, celebrating, maybe even crying and feeling something. Additionally, including a recipe with each story was a strategic part of the plan. There is nothing that connects us more than food, even at the most basic level. This component felt like a natural fit. On the other hand, the theme of baking, comes from my undeniable sweet tooth. Plus, baking has been shown to lead to improved self-esteem, increased concentration, coordination and confidence.

The overall goal of the book *Bake it Till You Make it: Breaking Bread, Building Resilience* in both process and purchase is to connect people. To allow a book to go from a shelf to a personal place of comfort and healing. To find a way to identify with others and to know, no matter how isolated you feel, you are not alone. Because life gets hard and as much as we know in our hearts that there are people there to support us, there is nothing like hearing this message from someone who has been there. Or at least I know this is how it was and still is, for me.

Today in 2019, I proclaim myself an open book but that was not always the case. Rather, this began after the Summer of 2011. I had just lived through the hardest summer of my life. I spent a total of 8 weeks in mental health treatment after my freshman year of college. While I saw pictures of beach vacations, parties and bonfires on Facebook, my reality looked more like structured meals, therapeutic homework and coloring pages. Although that summer took a lot from me, it gave me a voice.

Prior to 2011, I worked day in and day out to appear "happy". Growing up in a high achieving town, ridden with perfectionistic tendencies I wanted to do nothing but fit in. This was hard for me though, having been bullied and ditched by my friend group in 8th grade, I entered a new regional high school relatively alone. Things were not great at home either, which is something I still struggle to talk about. My world was closing in on me in all ways and my mask never came off. Ironically enough, I was nominated for "happiest" as a senior superlative when really, I was crumbling inside.

I always speak of the beginning of college as the "end of my apparent normalcy" as this life change really unleashed my demons to no end. It has taken me a long time to come to terms with this time in my life; as I feel for that scared, 18-year-old me. I had virtually no coping skills, no grasp on what was happening to me and no voice. Luckily, I made some amazing friends during my first week of college, who knew I needed help and they assisted me in accessing it. I found a therapist who understood me and still is one of the most special people in my life. I am grateful for not only everything she has taught me but the way she changed me. But even with her help, I continued to struggle throughout the next year and a half with my deteriorating mental health. Every time I thought I hit rock bottom, I fell another one thousand feet. This culminated in leaving my 10:30AM Western Civilization class one cold January morning, as an attempt to end my life in the closest bathroom. A medical leave ensued as did months on the couch in the same pajamas, occasionally brushing my teeth. One of my parents needed to stay home with me at all times, and it made me feel like the biggest burden to my family. I was so lost. No one else seemed to be struggling like me, or at least no one was talking about it. My peers were worried about formal dresses and grade point averages while 19 year old me was just trying to stay "positive." Having gained a voice during the months before my medical leave, I hit the ground running to make waves in the world even when I was still at my lowest. My sister and I started our own organization called "The BEA(YOU)TIFUL Project" that was dedicated to redefining beauty standards and supporting the National Eating Disorders Association. Advocacy was a huge part of what helped me sustain that voice and want to see another day, each day.

In March 2012, my life changed. I got off the waiting list for a prestigious treatment program after three months on academic medical leave. I no longer had to sit at home counting down the days when things were going to change, because I knew this would help me. I still remember what I wore the day of my turning point, the moment when I met with my hospital case manager at that time and therapist of now seven years, Dena. Yes the treatment program really helped as I loved the type of therapy I was exposed to but really it was (and still is) the bond and relationship I have with Dena that has kept me healing and believing in my ability to overcome anything I may face.

Ultimately, I applied and transferred to a new university; I didn't think I could ever walk back on that original campus. While the new school was a larger and in turn, "scarier", the match fit like

III

a glove.

My depression, eating disorder and obsessive compulsive disorder followed me into this new chapter but I was in a place where I could live with them all even while they were taking up real estate in my head. Things felt good and the "happy" mask continued to lift off as I began to realize there is so much more to me than being the "nice" or "happy" girl I thought I was nothing without.

In December of 2013, I left the country for the first time on Birthright. Birthright gives people ages 18-26 who are Jewish the opportunity to go to Israel for 10 days on a free trip. Being Jewish has always been important to me. Throughout my life, the high Jewish holidays were celebrated at my house, and my great grandfather always instilled the importance of Jewish values. Going on Birthright felt like a very meaningful opportunity. While I was there, I was taken advantage of, groomed, and ultimately, sexually assaulted. I lost my voice again. My first points of contact after that only added to the time that it took for me to feel safe in sharing again.

After this experience, I was so confused. I couldn't feel anything, so I would wash my hands with burning hot water. I laid on the floor of my apartment and cried for hours. I wanted to heal quickly, but it took a long time. Regaining my voice is still happening in this respect, but advocacy played a huge role yet again. As a result, I created a second organization "Erasing Excuses", created events and discussion platforms as well as my documentary *Life After: The Film* as a result.

Graduation tears put a new meaning to "water works" as there were so many moments between September 2010 and May 2015 that made graduating college feel impossible. So many moments believing I would live my life as a revolving door hospital patient or otherwise unfulfilled. The worst felt over and in a way this truly felt like the close on this chapter.

After graduating from college on a Friday, I started work on a Monday at the same hospital I received treatment at. This was my dream job, but I felt surprisingly underwhelmed. After about a year and half working at the hospital, I went back to school to get my Master's Degree. Working where I was treated was not the right fit for me for many reasons, but in ways I didn't expect. The job did not trigger me as I had feared, but felt like a stuck point. So I went back to school! Pursuing my Master's in Public Health and trying to do so in a year and a half, put a lot of pressure on my shoulders, the old demons were there again but new ones too. Every semester I felt like I was racing against my brain's clock escaping what felt like too much. Having faced an experience of a second sexual assault, second round of partial eating disorder treatment, those years were tough. However, great things came from graduate school too: new jobs, new adult-ing experiences, furthering my education, new connections, my documentary, a third organization, "Changing the Tape" as well as the beginning of *Bake it Till You Make It*.

Being almost a year out of grad school and reflecting on my story I recognize I am now in a new place. This doesn't mean projects are not still my life line or that I started drinking hot coffee by any means (iced all year round) but days are more predictable, especially because I love my job at Girls Inc. of Lynn. I have refined my friend group, Marie Kondo style, by prioritizing those who "spark joy", connection and love to me. As proud as I am to have reached this point, especially while being an outspoken advocate and activist, it was not until I embarked on creating this book that I truly felt connected. You see, authenticity used to be very lonely for me and it still can be. As my therapist Dena says, I was "vulnerable before it was trendy" and for no other reason than it organically inspired me.

Don't get me wrong, I love being transparent in hopes to help others as well as fight the stigma that surrounds mental health but the work can be isolating. And as much as I preach the importance of asking for help, it is hard.

But the book has brought me great company, sitting with the stories in the cookbook and realizing I am not alone. Whether the person shares their wisdom, support or their story, creating this book and learning about what vulnerability means to others has reignited a passion and love in me, and I want everyone to experience this when they open the book.

So take solace in the fact that you are not alone, that representation of how you are feeling is at your fingertips and that being human connects our imperfections, vulnerabilities and experiences in a way we could never imagine. In essence, you are human, welcome to the club! We all make mistakes, have a full range of emotions and I hope this book inspires you to keep fighting, to keep believing in yourself and keep reaching out.

Thank you for letting me take you there!

Love,
Your fellow perfectly imperfect also human and enthusiastic author

Dayna

Dedication

I can so easily think of and justify the dedication for this book to just about anyone in my life. From the amazing to the haters to my support system...but if I did that I would truly be missing the person who deserves the dedication, me. So, thank you, Dayna (me) for never giving up on your voice or this project. This is dedicated to the strength you have found, your unbelievable resilience, the innate super powers you have and the person you are.

Foreword

Dena B Tranen, LCSW

Bake it Till You Make It is a mental health cookbook offering the reader heartwarming and inspirational stories about living with and overcoming mental health challenges. This book provides recipes for making desserts and making life work while living with mental illness.

The title *Bake it Till You Make It* is clever twist on the saying "Fake it till you make it," an expression now seamlessly woven into our everyday vernacular, suggesting that if we act as if we have confidence or feel good, we can create that reality for ourselves. This idea is based somewhat on the work of nineteenth century German philosopher Hans Vaihinger, and was later used to inform Alfred Adler in developing therapeutic techniques such as roleplay. "Fake it till you make it" is a commonly used saying in AA and substance abuse recovery circles to encourage those who are newly sober to continue with the program even if their minds and bodies tell them they want to use again.

Act as if it is your reality and it will become your reality – this works for many people but, not surprisingly, it presented a bit of a dilemma for Dayna. After working with Dayna for many years, I know that she does authenticity better than pretending. Dayna is a strong and committed advocate for those struggling with their mental health. She uses her own story to show people that it's okay to talk about mental illness, it's okay to struggle, and it's okay to have days when you just can't fake it.

Bake it Till You Make It is more than a catchy title. This book offers inspiration, ideas and resources. By finding an activity such as baking or another hobby or vocation that we enjoy, we build a sense of self-efficacy and accomplishment. We don't have to fake it because the sense of achievement comes with the activity. Mental illness takes a lot from those who struggle with it. Baking, exercising, crafting, etc. allow us to give back to ourselves some of what was taken.

Many people living with mental illness have to fake it a lot of the time. They mask, they hide, and they downplay the pain they are in. *Bake it Till You Make It* is a huge step forward in the movement to reduce the stigma around mental health.

I am very proud of you, Dayna!

Bake it Til You Make it: Breaking Bread, Building Resilience

by Dayna Altman

TABLE OF CONTENTS

     I.   Ask the Psychiatric Mental Health Nurse Practitioner, Stacy Veo
          Paleo Chocolate Chip Cookies
     II.   Ask the Cousins, Jill Feinberg-Fishkin and Barbra Salerno
          Monkey Bread
     III.   Ask the Best Friend, Brenna Stewart
          Carrot Cake
     IV.   Ask the Friends who have been there, Abby Sullivan and Cara DiPietro
          Semi-Homemade Apple Pie
     V.   Ask the Teacher, Stephen Godbout
          Blueberry Ricotta Muffins
     VI.   Ask the Mom, Sheryl Altman
          Graham Cracker Brownies
     VII. Ask the Health Care Professionals, Gillian Praetorius and Emily Gibbs
          Heath Bar Scones
     VIII. Ask the Florida Grandmother, Leslie Parrino
          Coconut Cake

    I. Steph
        Mud Pie
    II. Jade Dube
        Cinnamon Swirls
    III. Ally Sexton-Thomas
        Peppermint Patty Brownies
    IV. Michelle S.
        Cheesecake
    V. Kayla Yates
        Healthy Banana Bread

What is a Mental Health Hotline?

A Mental Health Hotline is a free phone service that helps individuals in crisis - as well as support systems - access real time support by providing nearby resource recommendations and referrals to mental health providers in the community. These hotlines are available to anyone experiencing a mental health challenge, regardless of their health insurance status. Trained volunteers and staff members respond to these hotlines 24 hours a day, 7 days a week, 365 days a year.

In addition to phone hotlines, there are also Crisis Text Services which provide the same support services through text messaging.

Why use a hotline?

Hotlines can be accessed any time. Hotlines are answered by compassionate, trained professionals who are knowledgeable about relevant resources and able to provide in-the-moment suggestions for crisis management. Hotlines are not a replacement for counseling, but they are a supplemental support and can be accessed after hours when mental health professionals and providers may be otherwise unreachable.

What should you expect when calling a hotline?

While not all hotlines operate the same way, you can always expect to speak with a trained professional who will listen, support you, and suggest resources. Many national hotlines will route you to a local center, so you may have a few brief moments of waiting for a connection. Some hotlines may also ask you for a call back number if you get disconnected, or ask you for your first name. However, if you don't feel comfortable sharing those details, you don't have to. There are also many multilingual crisis workers, as well as support for the hearing impaired to help meet all callers' needs.

HOTLINES

National Suicide Prevention Lifeline (phone line)

1-800-273-8255

Crisis Text Line

Text NAMI to 741-741

*NAMI - National Alliance on Mental Illness

National Domestic Violence Helpline
1-800-799-7233

National Council on Alcoholism and Drug Dependence
1-800-622-2255

National Eating Disorder Association (NEDA) Help Line
1-800-931-2237

Part 1

Ask the...

Nurse Practitioner Stacy Veo's
Paleo Chocolate Chip Cookies

Ingredients:

- 1 cup blanched almond flour
- ¼ cup coconut flour
- 1 teaspoon baking soda
- ¼ teaspoon salt
- 6 tablespoons coconut oil or unsalted butter, room temperature
- ¾ cup coconut sugar or brown sugar
- 6 tablespoons natural almond butter, room temperature
- 1 and ½ teaspoons vanilla extract
- 1 large egg, room temperature (or 1 chia egg for vegan)
- 1 and ¼ cups semi-sweet chocolate chip

Notes to add my own voice to this recipe!

Directions

1. Preheat oven to 350F and line a baking sheet with parchment paper.

2. In a medium mixing bowl. stir together the almond flour. coconut flour. baking soda. and salt. Set aside.

3. In a large mixing bowl. beat together the fat and sugar at medium speed until well combined. If you use coconut oil. it may not come together easily. so use your hands to combine and then beat for another 20 seconds.

4. Beat in almond butter and vanilla extract on medium speed until combined.

5. Beat in egg on low and mix until well incorporated. then stir in flour mix.

6. Stir in I cup of chocolate chips. If you used brown sugar. skip to the next step. If you used coconut sugar. place the bowl in the refrigerator for about I hour or until the dough is firm.

7. Roll the dough into 8 balls and place the remaining ¼ cup of chocolate chips on the top and on the sides of the dough balls.

8. Place 4 inches apart on the prepared baking sheet. Press the cookies down lightly with the palm of your hand.

9. Bake for 11-14 minutes (if using coconut sugar) or 14-17 minutes (if using brown sugar) or until the center of the cookies no longer appears wet.

10. The cookies will be very soft but will continue to cook as they sit on the cookie sheet. Let cool completely on the baking sheet.

Q. My friend is struggling with their mental health; how can I help them?

A: I am big advocate for listening. I think you are the greatest help to someone by just being a neutral ear. It is important not to pass judgement (as I always say: I am not the judge or jury). For this reason, only when asked for advice or an opinion will I offer my perspective unless, I feel that person is struggling with something severe and needs immediate intervention, then all I can do is listen and provide referrals when warranted or asked. A huge piece of support is letting your friend know where your boundaries begin and end. For this reason, it's important to know where the resources are in your area, should they need to seek professional help.

Q. Why is there a stigma around mental health and taking medication?

A: This is such a big issue, unfortunately. I think this stigma was established long ago when people who were diagnosed with mental illness were transferred to psychiatric "wards" or hospitals rather than being present in their community seeking help. I also feel that society views mental health as something people can control instead of realizing that this is not the case. Mental illness is a disease much like that of heart disease, cancer, diabetes--these diseases are beyond a person's control and require treatment because they are debilitating or deadly. I always frame the issue of medication to my clients by saying: "If you had diabetes, would you take insulin to live?" Typically, (and I hope) the answer is always yes. I then will say, "then why wouldn't you treat your anxiety or depression, etc., as it is a disease of the brain."

Q. What is the most important ingredient in life?

A: Friends and family. These are your supports. They are the most important and valued people in your life. A good smile goes a long way too.

Q. If you could give one piece of advice to your younger self, what would it be?

A: Great question, oh man. I think it would be, "don't be so afraid to try new things or put yourself out there." I wish I had the confidence I have now when I was younger.

Q. Fill in the blank: I am not giving up on ____

A: Myself. In 33 years, many things have changed, I have changed. But I'm learning something new every day, taking every experience and mistake as a lesson towards building a better me.

BIO

Stacy Veo

Stacy Veo is a Lifespan Psychiatric Mental Health Nurse Practitioner. She is board certified with the American Nurses Credentialing Center and serves the child and adolescent populations, as well as the adults. She attended Worcester State University for her Bachelor of Science in Nursing, and worked as a Registered Nurse at a residential and day school program treating boys with emotional and behavioral issues. During this time, she earned her Master's Degree in Nursing, from Northeastern University. She is committed to providing comprehensive, quality care to her patients and their families. She enjoys spending time with her family and friends, traveling, and following her favorite Boston sports teams.

Notes, Thoughts & Goals

Two Cousin's Monkey Bread

Ingredients:

- 3 cans biscuits (10 per can)
- 1 cup sugar
- 3 tsp. cinnamon
- 1 tsp. brown sugar
- 1 stick (8 Tbsp.) butter

Optional
1 cup chocolate chips

Notes to add my own voice to this recipe!

Directions

1. Preheat the oven to 350f degrees.

2. Combine the sugar and cinnamon. Put mixture in large sealable plastic bag (e.g.. ziploc bag)

3. Cut each biscuit into four pieces. then throw the pieces in the cinnamon and sugar bag.

4. Take out the biscuits once covered in mixture and line the pieces in a bundt pan. Pour the remaining cinnamon and sugar into a measuring cup. Add brown sugar to make one cup.

5. Melt the butter and stir into the cinnamon and sugar mixture. Bring to a boil and then pour the mixture over the biscuits.

6. Bake for 40-45 minutes or until no longer doughy in the middle.

Jill

Q. What is the best part of this recipe?

A: I add chocolate chips to this monkey bread, which is absolutely the best part (highly recommend!)

Q. Why do you love it?

A: The best part of this recipe is that my mother used to make it. She emailed me the recipe so I could make it for my family and now the printed email has baked grounds in it. This is a recipe made of love.

Q. What gets you through the hardest challenges?

A: Exercise, family, listening to Hamilton.

Q. What would you say to someone who is struggling with their mental health?

A: While it may seem simple, I would encourage someone to think about special memories and "happy places." I would then suggest remembering those memories do not exist without you in them. And of course, to seek resources and support.

Q. What is the most important ingredient in life?

A: I can't say it enough: love. It is the most special ingredient in this recipe and in life.

Barbra

Q. What advice would you give someone who is struggling?

A: Hang in there. Life experiences might not work out the way you hoped and you can't always control the outcomes. But you always move on from difficult experiences. Always. That doesn't mean you forget, but you move on.

Q. What is the most important lesson you have learned in life?

A: Greatness comes from practice. Never, ever give up.

Q. I'm not giving up on____

A: My children. EVER.

Q. I believe in ____

A: Doing the right thing! I believe that it can be tempting to make poor decisions because it is easier but in the long run people will remember you for being honest.

BIO

Jill Feinberg-Fishkin

Jill lives in Baltimore with her husband. David. and two daughters. Stephanie (16) and Rebecca (13).

Barbra Salerno

Barbra lives in Massachusetts with her husband. Jay. and two sons. Max (14) and Charlie (12).

Jill Feinberg-Fishkin and Barbra Salerno are mothers. wives. sisters. daughters. and proud cousins of the cookbook's author. Jill and Barbra both love baking for their families. and always advise adding some extra chocolate chips to this recipe.

Notes, Thoughts & Goals

Ingredients:

- 2 cups flour
- 2 tsp. baking powder
- 1 tsp. baking soda
- 1½ tsp. ground cinnamon
- ½ tsp. ground ginger
- ¼ tsp. ground nutmeg
- ½ tsp. salt
- ¾ cup canola or vegetable oil
- 4 large eggs. room temperature
- 1½ cups light brown sugar
- ½ cup granulated sugar
- ½ cup unsweetened applesauce
- 1 tsp. pure vanilla extract
- 3 cups grated carrots. lightly packed

Cream Cheese Frosting:

- 1 package (8 oz.) brick-style cream cheese. softened to room temperature
- ½ cup (8 Tbsp.) unsalted butter. softened to room temperature
- 2 cups powdered sugar
- 1 tsp. pure vanilla extract

Directions

1. Preheat the oven to 350F degrees. Spray one 9-inch round cake pan well with non-stick cooking spray.

2. In a large mixing bowl. whisk together the flour. baking powder. baking soda. cinnamon. ginger. nutmeg. and salt until well combined. Set aside.

3. In a separate large mixing bowl. whisk together the oil. eggs. brown sugar. granulated sugar. applesauce. and vanilla extract until fully combined. Add the grated carrots into the wet ingredients and mix until well combined.

4. Pour the wet ingredients into the dry ingredients and mix with a whisk or rubber spatula until just combined. making sure not to over-mix the batter.

5. In the bowl of a stand mixer fitted with the paddle attachment. or in a large mixing bowl using a hand-held mixer. beat the cream cheese until smooth. Add the butter and mix for about 30-60 seconds until well combined and smooth. Add in the powdered sugar and vanilla extract. and continue mixing until fully combined. scraping down the sides of the bowl as needed. Put aside until the cake is baked and out of the oven.

6. Pour the cake batter evenly into the cake pan.

7. Bake for 30-35 minutes.

8. Let cool and add cream cheese frosting.

Q. What is the most beautiful part of holding on?

A: The good days. They're a nice reminder that although the good things in life are temporary, so are the bad. They inspire and motivate me to keep moving forward, and leave me excited for what good things are up ahead.

Q. What advice would you give someone who is struggling?

A: As cliché as it sounds, keep going. There is always someone out there rooting for you —- someone who will always see your best qualities, even when you don't. Believe this, and let them in.

Q. I'm not giving up on _____

A: Finding my purpose.

Q. The most important ingredient in life is _____

A: Kindness.

Author's note: Brenna truly is the kindest person I know. I am so grateful to have her in my life. Thank you for being my rock and person.

BIO

Brenna Stewart

Brenna Stewart is a recent graduate of University of Massachusetts Lowell, where she earned a BA in Psychology. Brenna currently works in the mental health setting, providing treatment and support to young women. Additionally, Brenna is a photographer: In fact, she took most of the photos featured in this book. She believes the beauty of photography is captured through the ability to look at life through a different lens. Brenna enjoys exploring new places with her camera and with her boyfriend, Ryan. Brenna continues to be a kind, compassionate, and talented person towards all who have the privilege of knowing her. Brenna is also the biggest Taylor Swift fan - maybe ever? If you are reading this, Taylor, you have your new bff on deck!

Friends Abby and Cara's Semi-Homemade Apple Pie

Ingredients:

- Pre-Made pie crust
- 1 ¼ cup of water
- 1 Tbsp. unsalted butter, melted
- 1 Tbsp. of butter, softened to room temperature
- 5-6 medium sized apples
- ¼ tsp. cinnamon
- Small spoonful of flour

Notes to add my own voice to this recipe!

Directions

1. Preheat the oven to 350F degrees.

2. This recipe is semi-homemade because you use a box of Pre-Made pie crust. but ignore the box instructions and add 1/4 cup water and a tablespoon of melted butter. Mix with a fork and roll out into two flat crusts. Place one crust into the pie pan.

3. Chop 5-6 medium sized apples into small pieces and add them on top of the bottom crust.

4. Make a mixture of 1 cup sugar. about 1/4 tsp cinnamon. and a small spoonful of flour. Spoon that mixture over the chopped apples.

5. Place a few small pats of butter over the apples. then top with the second crust.

6. Bake at 350F degrees for 45 minutes then at 400F degrees for 15 mins.

Both women have struggled with their own mental health challenges. Abby reports continuing to battle an anxiety disorder and Cara is currently in recovery from an eating disorder. They have both worked extremely hard to find a place where they can live full lives despite these disorders and candidly share their wisdom here.

Q. What has been your biggest struggle thus far?

A: [ABBY] As far back as I can remember, anxiety has been a lingerer in my life - whether manifested in the form of OCD, longer term stress or symptoms of depression. When I'm in "the dark" I remind myself there is light - and it's coming.

A: [CARA] My biggest struggle thus far has been coping with an eating disorder and the journey to recovery. I was diagnosed with an eating disorder in 2015, but it started long before that in 8th grade. There was never a specific moment but I remember being involved in a toxic friendship. This person was very manipulative and really isolated me from the rest of my friends. I handled this silencing experience by restricting my food. It started as a control thing and it wasn't about losing weight...however, that became a theme later. I think the hardest part of recovery is adjusting to a recovered body. Being in one body for so long and being used to it, makes you learn that a body can change.

Q. Was there one moment when you feel you shifted into recovery?

A: [ABBY] For me, it isn't black & white. It's not "you're sick with anxiety or you're cured." It's never linear, but super fluid. I've found the best way to live with anxious tendencies is to acknowledge them when they show up, thank them for coming, then kindly ask 'em to go away.

A: [CARA] Prom was a big night for me. Being at prom in a dress, eating dinner with my friends and not really caring about the food was huge. I have always said I want to eat cake on my wedding day and not feel guilty about it. Prom was the first step!

Q. What advice would you give to your younger self if you could?

A: [ABBY] When you are loved, you have it all. Too much of our time is spent focusing on the things we can't change (or on the aspects we can, yet still not changing 'em) and in measuring ourselves up to those we think 'have it all.' If you are loved, you already have it all. Don't question that, never take it for granted - and consider all else a bonus.

A: [CARA] I would want my younger self to know there are so many incredible things that you are able to experience in life if you choose recovery. It is funny-there are so many joyful moments that come when you start respecting yourself. I would want my younger self to remember that you only get so much time on this earth and your body is a beautiful tool to live it, so take advantage of that!

Q. You have overcome so much already, you are such an inspiration! What is next?

A: [ABBY] In my "old age" I've adopted a mentality of living for the day, not jumping ahead. Flexibility has been the most advantageous character trait I've practiced. When you plan too strictly and too far out, you panic when things don't follow suit. But when you're truly flexible, every curveball is just a new part of the journey.

A: [CARA] Ideally, I want to be an advocate in some way in terms of mental health and performing arts. I want to share my story and convey that I am proud that I chose recovery and you can too!

BIO

Abby Sullivan

Abby is a Northeastern University grad with a BA in journalism, and is currently working as Content Marketing Manager at ProfitWell, a Boston SaaS startup disrupting the subscription industry. Her skills include writing, bopping around new restaurants, and petting her dog, Charlie. She's a self-proclaimed food fanatic, happiest by the water and her family's side, eating hot dogs and reminiscing about their travels together, both near and far.

Cara DiPietro

Cara is currently a student at Elon University. Having grown up on stage, Cara has loved finding her voice, presence, and self through her art. In addition to her musical theater pursuits, Cara also plays the guitar, piano, and ukulele. A Massachusetts native, Cara loves spending time with her family and friends in between semesters, as well as time with her dog, Maisy.

Notes, Thoughts & Goals

Teacher Stephen Godbout's Blueberry Ricotta Muffins

Ingredients:

- 1½ cups all-purpose flour
- 1 cup sugar
- 2 tsp. baking powder
- Pinch of salt
- 3 eggs
- 1½ cups ricotta
- 1 tsp. vanilla extract
- 1 stick (8 Tbsp.) of unsalted butter melted
- 1½ cups frozen blueberries
- ½ cup Powdered Sugar
- Optional: Whipped cream

Notes to add my own voice to this recipe!

Directions

1. Preheat oven to 350f degrees.

2. Spray the minicake pan (or regular pan) with nonstick spray.

3. In one bowl. sift flour. sugar. salt. and baking powder.

4. In another bowl whisk the eggs together before adding the ricotta. vanilla and butter.

5. Slowly combine the wet ingredients into the dry. mixing well.

6. Fold in 1 cup of blueberries. trying not to break them up.

7. Sprinkle the rest of the blueberries on top.

8. Bake for about 35-40 minutes in mini-cake pan or 50-60 in the regular cake pan.

9. A toothpick or fork should come out clean when tested after baking.

10. Let cool. and sprinkle with powdered sugar. and additionally. suggest adding the optional whipped cream.

Q. What advice would you give to someone who is struggling with their mental health?

A: Talk to someone who has your very best interests in their heart and mind. Write, reflect, exhale.

Q. How, as a teacher and parent, have you worked to encourage the younger generations to "hold on" or "keep going" even when it may feel impossible?

A: Be true to yourself. I believe that in each of us there is a wanting, or calling, to press on and leave the world a better place than we found it. There's a kindness in each of us. The best part of being human is that we get to carry each other in hard times. When times are hard, someone is there to carry you and then you will be called upon to carry another.

Q. What are the stressors facing teens today?

A: Social media. It's such a strange landscape for kids to navigate. Old people like myself didn't have to endure all that comes with social media in our adolescence which was already difficult enough without it! Emotions run high during adolescence. I think (I honestly don't know because I'm not on social media) that kids want to identify with whatever other people on social media are feeling at any given time. That can be good and bad and there's no longitudinal evidence of what the outcomes may be. Based on my perspective, kids seem more stressed than ever these days and I believe social media has played a role in that escalation of stress and anxiety.

Q. The most important ingredient in life is: _____

A: Surround yourself with people who make you smile. Live, laugh, love! Exercise and live well.

There's a kindness in each of us.

BIO

Stephen Godbout

Stephen Godbout is a husband, dad, and teacher. He has had the privilege of having wonderful human beings like Dayna (the author of this book) in his classes over the years. Dayna has been sharing her journey with Stephen's classes for the last 5 years or so. When Dayna stopped by earlier this year, he profusely thanked her again. He was compelled to tell Dayna that she is a hero in the truest sense of the word: She is courageous, resilient, and a role model to all. Stephen says his life has been far less inspiring, but he finds fulfillment in family. He has an amazing wife, Barri Lynn, and together they are the proud parents of the most wonderful sons they could ask for. His hobbies include biking, skiing, and being around people who make him smile. When asked about his aspirations, Stephen responded, "Aspirations? Kindness. I have one classroom rule, 'Spread Kindness.' I try my best to encourage kindness in times like this when we need it most."

Notes, Thoughts & Goals

Mom Sheryl Altman's
Graham Cracker Brownies

Ingredients:

1 Box Graham Cracker Crumbs
2 Cans Evaporated condensed milk
2 Bags milk chocolate chips (can experiment with
   different types of chocolate chips as well)

Notes to add my own voice to this recipe!

Directions

1. Preheat the oven to 325f degrees.

2. Mix all ingredients together in a bowl until well blended.

3. Pour batter into a greased 13x9-inch pan.

4. Bake for 35 minutes.

They will come out "soupy" but will harden as they cool.

Q. What have you learned in your life thus far?

I am so honored to be a part of this cookbook and I am so proud of Dayna for taking on this project. From the time Dayna turned five, she has been taking on projects, created totally by her mind. When people (especially me) would say, "Dayna, you are only five! You cannot stage a full-scale musical in our basement or at the library" she would prove us wrong every time. From musicals, to dance shows, to creating mental health and advocacy organizations like The BEA[YOU]TIFUL Project, to her full scale fashion show, her documentary *Life After*, to a blog ...whatever she says she is going to do, she does; regardless of the obstacles.

Truly, no one can stop her. Dayna is always in motion. This project is especially meaningful to me because my great grandmother's family were bakers in Austria. When they came to the US they opened and ran a bakery for many years in, Brooklyn NY, so baking is in our DNA.

I'm also so proud of how Dayna has taken her challenges and struggles and turned them into something positive. Dayna has asked me to write something about mental health which is a little difficult for me since I tend to be very guarded but I want to support her so here I go.

I feel that I have had a lot of challenges and struggles with my mental health during the various chapters of my life as I look back now. As I lived through it, however, I feel that I buried a lot under the rug...staying quiet to make everyone else happy. So instead of facing the challenges, I buried them in goals.... whether it be college, law school, marriage and relationships, taking care of my children.

Now that my children are grown and I have time to reflect, many mental challenges have come to the surface which has made me think about what I have experienced. I am not ashamed to say that I have seen a therapist who has helped me heal the many traumas that I have experienced.

I realize now, finally that the key to healing is the realization and the reflection. The tapes will never change and the thoughts and patterns that do not serve us, will continue to haunt us unless they are dealt with directly.

I encourage anyone reading this to know that it's never too late to change! Or to heal, to change your vibrational energy and tap into a healthier happier life.

BIO

Sheryl Altman

Sheryl Altman is the proud mother of the author of this book. Originally from New York City. Sheryl now lives in Southborough. MA. with her husband. and is the mother of two amazing daughters: one on the East Coast and one on the West Coast. On most days. you can find her singing her heart out. teaching Bikram yoga and Pilates. or "lawyering" over contracts.

Notes, Thoughts & Goals

Health Care Pros Gillian and Emily's Heath Bar Scones

Ingredients:

- 2 cups flour
- ¼ cup + 2 Tbsp. sugar
- 1 Tbsp. baking powder
- ½ tsp. salt
- ½ cup of mini chocolate chips
- ½ cup toffee bits
- 1 ¼ cup whipped cream
- 3 Tbsp. unsalted butter

Notes to add my own voice to this recipe!

Directions

1. Preheat oven to 425F degrees.

2. Combine flour. 1/4 cup sugar. baking powder. and salt in a large bowl.

3. Stir in chocolate chips and toffee bits. Add whipped cream.
   Stir until dough firms.

4. Turn onto a floured surface and knead lightly. just until dough holds together. Form into a circle that is 10 inches in. diameter and a ½-inch thick.

5. Cut into 12 pie-shaped wedges and transfer to a baking sheet.

6. Brush tops of wedges with melted butter and sprinkle on remaining 2 tablespoons of sugar.

7. Bake for 10-15 minutes until golden brown. Cool on wire rack

Q. Why is caring for your mental health important?

A: [Gillian] As a nurse, I see firsthand how mental and physical health are intertwined, and one cannot exist without the other. Just like how a person can develop emotional concerns when struggling with a medical condition, excessive worrying and negative thoughts can be dangerous to one's physical health. Mental health is much broader that people realize, and it's not just relevant to those with diagnosed psychiatric illnesses; it's relevant to everyone. We've all been told that in order to stay physically healthy, we need to eat well, exercise, and see our doctor. It's just as important to take care of your mental health and everyone will have a different way of doing that. Whether it's journaling, quieting your mind, or baking, finding something that is calming and adds value to your life is critical. Mental health is essential to your well-being, so make it a daily priority to take care of yourself because you are worthy of self-love and respect.

A: [Emily] As someone who works in healthcare, identifying one's own key "ingredients" for life is important. Here are mine:

• Family: It is everything to me and I have learned that as I get older, now, more than ever.

• Love: I truly believe it can bring anything and anyone into your life.

• Friend: They make everything I do worthwhile.

• Happiness: Because it is worth fighting for.

Friends: They make everything I do worthwhile.

BIO

Gillian Praetorius

Gillian Praetorius is a lifelong best friend of the author, Dayna. An Emergency Department charge nurse at a large hospital, Gillian works hard to keep the community healthy and provide the best care she can to anyone who comes into the ER overnight. Gillian has been a Registered Nurse for the last few years, after graduating with her degree in 2014 from Quinnipiac University. Gillian loves to travel and explore new places, especially with her boyfriend, Tyler. She loves to ski with her family, bake with her friends, and appreciate the time with those in her life. She also helped design and display some of the food photos in this book - maybe a new hobby?

Emily Gibbs

Emily Gibbs graduated from Northeastern University in 2015 with a degree in Health Science and Business Management. She currently lives in New York and works at the Hospital for Special Surgery, after working previously at Boston Children's Hospital post-graduation. Emily loves spending time with her family, and spending any time she can on the beach... as she always says: "Time wasted on a beach is time well spent."

Notes, Thoughts & Goals

Florida Grandmother Leslie's Coconut Cake

Ingredients:

Cake
- 1 ½ flour
- 1 cup granulated sugar
- 2 cups milk or water
- 1 Tbsp. shortening
- 1 tsp. vanilla
- 1 egg

Topping
- ½ cup flaked coconut
- 1/3 cup packed brown sugar
- ¼ cup of chopped nuts
- 3 Tbsp. unsalted butter. softened
- 2 Tbsp. milk

Notes to add my own voice to this recipe!

Directions

1. Pre-heat the oven to 350f degrees.

2. Grease and flour 9-inch round cake pan or 8-inch square pan.

3. In a large bowl. beat flour. granulated sugar. 6 cup milk or water. shortening. vanilla. and egg with an electric mixer on low speed 30 seconds. scraping the bowl constantly. Beat on medium speed 4 minutes. scraping the bowl occasionally. Pour into the pan.

4. Bake 30-35 minutes or until toothpick inserted in center comes out clean: Cool slightly.

5. In a small bowl. mix coconut. brown sugar. nuts. butter and 2 tablespoons of milk. Spread this topping over the cake. Set oven to broil. Broil about 3 inches from heat for about 3 minutes or until golden brown.

Q. What is a lesson you have learned over your life that you wish to share?

A: When I was attending High School, I was very shy and had a hard time fitting in. I was a very good student but had trouble in social situations. Even though I was nervous to do so, I thought joining a club would be a way to help alleviate the isolation I felt. Even though it was hard at first, this step helped bring me confidence and gave me a way to relate to others. I never got to the point where it was necessarily easy for me and I know it is an obstacle I will continue to need to overcome. However, I have found so much value in social connection and know it is a key part of life. Connection is also vital to your happiness and in building support. If this sounds like you, take a leap of faith and try something new: it might be scary but you never know what that push outside of your comfort zone could bring. I am now in my 70s and travel often. I have made such meaningful connections and memories since I decided to push myself.

Take a leap of faith and try something NEW.

BIO

Leslie Parrino

Leslie Parrino, originally from New York, is now enjoying life in sunny Sarasota, Florida. She spent most of her career as a Probation Officer in New York City. She loves theater and now volunteers as an usher at local shows. She also enjoys tennis, foreign films, and of course, traveling and exploring.

Notes, Thoughts & Goals

General Statistics

KEY TERMS TO UNDERSTAND DATA

All data has been drawn from the National Institute of Mental Health (NIMH)

Two types of mental illness defined in the data:

1. **Any Mental Illness (AMI): mental illness that ranges in severity, this "catch-all term" is used to illustrate a mental, emotional, or behavioral disorder that impacts one's life.**
2. **Serious Mental Illness (SMI): a subset of AMI, depicting severe interference in one's normal life, usually captured by talking about those who "experience disability." (NIHM 2018)**

Fast Facts

About 1 in 5 adults lives with a mental illness. (NIH 2016)

About 31.1% of the U.S. adult population will experience an anxiety disorder diagnosis at some point in their lifetime. (NIH 2016)

Major depression is one of the most common mental health disorders in the U.S. About 12.1%, or 3.1 million, adolescents in the U.S. were said to have at least one depressive episode. (NIH 2016)

Death by suicide is the **tenth** leading cause of death in the U.S. for adults and the **second** leading cause of death for those ages 10-34. (NIH 2016)

Most people who suffer from personality disorders (over 80%) also are diagnosed with a co-occurring disorder. (NIH 2016)

Schizophrenia is one of the top causes of disability worldwide. (NIH 2016)

Citation

National Institute of Mental Health (2018) National Survey (2016) Bethesda, MD. https://www.nimh.nih.gov/health/statistics/

Part 2

From the Kitchen of Survivors

Steph M's Mud Pie

Ingredients:

- 1 container coffee ice cream softened
- 1 jar hot fudge
- 1 jar caramel sauce
- 2 containers cool whip

Notes to add my own voice to this recipe!

Directions

1. In a 13 x 9 pan spread container of coffee ice cream.

2. Cover ice cream with the full jar of hot fudge creating an even layer on top of ice cream.

3. Cover hot fudge layer with full jar of caramel sauce.

4. Cover caramel sauce with both containers of cool whip.

5. Freeze for 30 minutes until firm.

Content Warning: OCD, Eating Disorder

1. I am an undercover basket case. I am neurotic. I am obsessive, and I am compulsive. I am a control freak, an extreme creature of habit, and a pain to live with. I need my room immaculate, and I will not get into an unmade bed under any circumstances. I have become an expert in hiding how I really feel.

2. In elementary school, I was "that kid" who brought my own sets of colored pencils to hide in my desk because the thought of other students not re-sharpening them or not keeping them in perfect rainbow order repulsed me.

3. In high school, I was "that sister" who secretly panicked when my younger sister Allie turned sixteen because I feared that she would leave our shared car messy when she drove it.

4. In college, I was "that roommate" in my apartment who hid my favorite coffee mug in my bedroom because I was scared that, if I were to leave it in the kitchen cabinet, someone would take it, use it, and then not clean it.

5. I am, and always will be, "that person." After living with diagnosed obsessive-compulsive disorder for eleven years, I have come to accept it. I suppose one would not guess that this is a daily struggle for me. I try to maintain a sunny disposition and genuinely attempt to see the positive in every situation.

6. I also recognize that if I were to let my actual emotional turmoil show every time one of my roommates left a crumbled paper towel on the counter in my apartment, or every time they left a drawer open or a dish in the sink, I probably would have been friendless and homeless.

7. When I was ten, my mom told me that she was taking me to see a "feelings doctor." A feelings doctor, she explained, was just like my pediatrician, but was there to help me with how my mind was feeling instead of how my body was working.

8. At this time, my dad was suffering from congestive heart failure, a condition in which the heart doesn't pump blood as well as it should. While he was in the hospital undergoing surgery, the surgeon made a mistake and nicked my dad's esophagus, which resulted in sepsis. My dad had already spent over a month in the intensive-care unit of Brigham and Womens' Hospital in Boston. A few days before my first trip to "the feelings doctor," whom I will from now on call "the therapist," my dad had his last rites read to him. While part of my mom's reasoning for taking me to therapy was to prepare me for the fact that it was highly likely I was about to lose my father, she was also noticing some strange patterns in my behavior. It was the first time in my life that I remembered feeling completely helpless. I had no idea what was going to happen to my dad, or how we would go on without him. I began cleaning my room for over an hour each day, writing and re-writing every homework assignment, and washing my hair twice before conditioning. My ten-year-old self believed that completing these routines would help my dad get better. I was diagnosed with OCD that same year.

9. Truth be told, I blocked out a lot of what happened when my dad was sick. I was also too young to fully comprehend the medical terminology and what was really happening to him. One small memory I do recall is the time I watched him pass out in our upstairs hallway after being out of the hospital for a few days, only to be taken away again in an ambulance.

10. Though I did not grow up in a religious household, having been raised by a Jewish mother and a Roman Catholic father, both of whom cared more about being good people than enforcing the doctrine of a specific belief system, I remember my dad giving me his cross and his medals of Saint Anthony- the saint of both healing and the recovery of lost items. I think he had intended for me to keep them if he were to pass away. These medals held no particular religious meaning to me, yet I wore them every single day while my dad was in the hospital. I wanted part of him with me wherever I went. To this day, one of the best days of my life was when I gave him back those medals.

11. Even after my dad recovered, I stayed in therapy for a while. My neurotic behavior had not gone away overnight. Eventually, I stopped seeing a therapist and only saw a guidance counselor when needed for the rest of elementary and middle school. By high school, I felt as if I were "normal" again.

12. I made all A's and was in the top ten percent of my class. I ran cross-country even though I almost always placed third to last in meets (which did not bother me -- I was never an athlete). I had a solid group of friends. My need for control began to increase, though, with the approach of junior year. College-talk had begun, and the consequential competitive climate that came with these conversations started to worry me.

13. My bedroom, again, became my avenue to a sense of control. I had dreamed for my entire life of going to the University of Michigan. Though I can now happily say that I obtained the ninth University of Michigan degree in my family, the uncertainty I felt my last two years of high school that centered on not knowing the status of my admission scared me. I Clorox-wiped my desk each night before I began my homework and again after I completed it. I could not study unless my bed was perfectly made -- my white monogrammed pillowcases with pink lettering pristinely arranged to look like a Pottery Barn catalogue. I color-coded my closet and cleaned out my drawers to make sure that every t-shirt I owned was folded properly. There was a place for everything and everything was in its place. Always. Should my room not align with this status of perfection, I would break down.

14. Perfection (or more realistically the appearance of perfection) was the norm in my hometown, and having OCD made me put even more pressure on myself to appear "perfect."
My parents had noticed my intensified obsessive behavior though, and gently suggested to me that it might be time for me to revisit therapy. If I had not listened to my parents, I would have never met Kathy.

15. While at first I had a difficult time sharing with Kathy, I quickly learned how easy it was to talk to her. I had imagined that therapy would suck. I pictured trying to open up to a total stranger, only to have him or her ask me "how I felt about that" after every sentence that would come out of my mouth.

16. Don't get me wrong, therapy sometimes did suck. There were times where I couldn't even drive myself home because I was so emotionally exhausted. But with Kathy, it was different, and I viewed my emotional exhaustion as progress. Kathy was the coolest. She ran her practice out of her house and always had a different vinyl on display in her waiting room. Kathy was all about embracing our quirks and accepting who we are. She taught me how to overcome the ridiculous pressure I put on myself and to accept that we can't control everything around us. When I graduated high school, she gave me the most beautiful LC Secretarial typewriter because she knew I had a passion for collecting antiques. I learned so much from Kathy, but most importantly I learned how to look at myself for more than just my flaws and what I could control.

17. When I went off to college, I felt well prepared. Kathy told me that she would take appointments by Facetime if I ever needed her. I genuinely felt as though I had become less uptight by the end of senior year, and I was more than ready to move 790 miles away.

18. About a quarter way through my freshman year, I again began to feel as though my grip was slipping on my reign of control. I had quickly learned that "neat" is an incredibly subjective term; the adjustment to sharing a cramped dorm room was more difficult than I had anticipated. This time, however, I didn't have my own bedroom to clean. I couldn't just touch someone else's stuff, and my side of the room was already spotless. I needed another outlet.

19. I spent the nights of my freshman year in the basement bathroom of my dorm. It was a single stall bathroom, set in the corner of the rarely occupied lounge, which allowed optimal privacy. I knew what I was doing was wrong -- but it made me feel as though I could be enough. Bulimia for me was a new path of control. If I couldn't control my own body, what else did I have?

20. My compulsive cleaning had once filled a void in my life. Observing my clean room with everything in its place (from the throw pillows to my color-coded closet) made me feel put-together, even when everything else seemed to be falling apart. My clean space made me feel enough for myself because I knew that I always had some sense of control over my environment. I guess controlling what came in and out of my body had a similar effect.

21. I wrote earlier about how the best day of my life was giving my dad back his medals. One of the worst days of my life was seeing my mom's reaction when she found out I had dealt with bulimia for most of freshman year.

22. I was eighteen years old, but I had begged my mom come with me to my yearly physical at the doctor's office in case I had to get a shot.

23. We waited for the doctor. My mom joked that if I had to get a shot she would get me a Starbucks if I were brave.

24. I got weighed; my mom stood behind me looking at the number on the scale. Knowing nothing, she mentioned how great I looked.

25. The doctor began to ask me about my adjustment to college, whether my birth control was still working, and if I had noticed any behavioral changes since being put on a stronger dose of my antidepressant.

26. "Have you ever, in any way, tried to harm yourself?"

27. I paused, beginning to pick at my dry cuticles.

28. My mom looked up from the game of solitaire she had been mindlessly playing on her phone.

29. The doctor repeated the question, this time looking me directly in the eye and listing behaviors that classify as self-harm.

30. "...cutting, burning, starving yourself or inducing vomit."

31. Hearing the last example, I averted my gaze. In that moment, the doctor and my mom both knew. Sitting in that sterile-smelling, ugly-wallpapered nine by six cell, the walls closed in on me. My mouth felt dry; my heart felt heavy.

32. I started to cry. So did she.

33. I have since recovered from my eating disorder, and in all honesty, I hadn't fully recognized that my behavior qualified as disordered eating until that day in the doctor's office. I had never viewed what I was doing as means to reach an end goal, but rather as something that would allot me control. I, of course, went back to Kathy and spoke about it with her a great deal. I later learned that bulimia is tied closely to OCD. Both involve compulsive behavior and a need for control.

34. While it is true that I have struggled with control issues for over half of my life, I have also been lucky enough to have surrounded myself with incredible people who support me throughout every bad day, as well as every good day. My friends and family encourage me to be myself, and accept me for everything that "myself" entails. My parents have even allowed me to create an art room in my basement, a room in which I can paint all over the walls and healthily relieve my stress.

35. My parents have also instilled in me a value in self-awareness that has allowed me to (slowly, but surely) see the good in my OCD. At fourteen, I was too young to legally obtain a job, and I had complained to them that I wanted to work. With their encouragement and gas mileage, I went to Staples, purchased business cards, and started "Steph's Simple Solutions." That entire summer, I charged my neighbors in exchange for my de-cluttering services, and study-skills lessons for their kids.

36. It's actually a great story to tell in job interviews, and I believe my organization skills have helped me to obtain some pretty incredible internships. Even now, I sometimes joke that my agenda will always be my best friend, only aside from Clorox wipes. Yes, I one hundred percent realize how pathetic that sounds, but you would be surprised at how many people love that line.

37. I am an undercover basket case. I am neurotic. I am obsessive, and I am compulsive. I am a control freak, an extreme creature of habit, and a pain in the ass to live with. I need my room immaculate and I will not get into an unmade bed under any circumstances. I've come to understand that my OCD is something that will never completely go away. I know that it does not define me, but that in some ways, it will always shape who I am. I find solace in channeling my need for control by collecting antique cameras and typewriters (and have used my superb organizational skills to display all twenty-eight of these keepsakes beautifully on a shelf in my room). I have learned to take refuge in my art courses, a space in which I can safely let go of control. I am unique outside of my neuroticism but also because of it.

BIO

Steph M.

Steph is a young professional living and working in New York City. She is a Digital Media Planner by day and a friend, role model, SoulCycle warrior, writer and travel enthusiast on her own time. Steph is a graduate of the University of Michigan and originally from Massachusetts. The recipe she contributed is a long-term favorite of her family as well as Dayna's (the author) family. Steph and Dayna have great memories of enjoying this dessert together; along with their families, every Jewish holiday. Over the years, Steph and her sister Allie became more like family then friends to Dayna and her sister, Jamie. She will always be grateful for the sisterhood among the four girls.

Jade D's Cinnamon Swirls

Ingredients:

- 2.5 cups flour
- 2 Tbsp. sugar
- 12 Tbsp. unsalted butter, cold (chopped into several slices)
- ½ cup shortening, cold (cut in four pieces)
- ¼ cup vodka
- ¼ cup cold water
- 8 Tbsp. unsalted butter, melted
- 2 Tbsp. cinnamon
- ½ cup of sugar

Notes to add my own voice to this recipe!

Directions

1. Preheat the oven to 350f degrees.

2. In a food processor, add 1 6 cups of flour and 2 tablespoons of sugar. Pulse briefly to combine.

3. Slowly add in the pieces of cold butter and shortening, and pulse the food processor when adding in these ingredients. The dough will look like cottage cheese.

4. Add in the rest of the flour, and pulse until smooth.

5. Take the dough out of the current bowl, and in a separate bowl, add the vodka and water to the dough.

6. Refrigerate dough for 30 mins to allow it to compact.

7. Take dough out of the fridge and roll out on a smooth surface.

8. Cut the dough into strips, and roll each strip from one end to the other, into a spiral shape, laying the finished product flat on the surface of the pan.

9. Brush a few teaspoons of melted butter on the dough. In a small separate bowl, combine the cinnamon and sugar.

10. Sprinkle the mixture of cinnamon and sugar on the dough "swirl".

11. Bake for 45 minutes or until browned.

Content Warning:
Borderline Personality Disorder, Bipolar Disorder

When people think of mental illness, they get scared. When I tell people that I have borderline personality disorder and bipolar disorder, they look at me differently. I was hospitalized twice for suicide attempts and severe self-harm. I have lost friends because of the diagnosis and my actions. People began to treat me like I was fragile, and in the beginning, I was. For a long time, I was in a very bad place and was devastated by my diagnosis. I thought it would define my life. Living with these disorders is not easy, but what really helps me is thinking about the lessons I learned from figure skating. I was a competitive figure skater for 13 years and was ranked in the top ten in New England. What I loved about skating was that each time I stepped onto the ice, I got to create a new story. And that is now how I look at each day: a clean sheet of ice.

I got to create a new story.

BIO

Jade Dube

Jade Dube is a graduate student studying Social Work at Bridgewater State University in Bridgewater. MA. She aspires to work in the mental health field and become a therapist. When she is not in classes or studying. she works with individuals with traumatic brain injuries. Jade loves walking her dogs and catching up on the most recent skating competitions.

Notes, Thoughts & Goals

Ally's Peppermint Patty Brownies

Ingredients:

- 1 1/2 cups unsalted butter or margarine
- 3 cups white sugar (or equivalent sugar substitute)
- 1 Tbsp. vanilla extract
- 5 eggs
- 2 cups all-purpose flour (or flour substitute)
- 1 tsp. salt
- 1 tsp. baking powder
- 1 cup unsweetened cocoa powder
- 24 small peppermint patties

Notes to add my own voice to this recipe!

Directions

1. Preheat oven to 350f degrees.

2. Mix the butter. sugar. and vanilla in large bowl.

3. Beat in the eggs.

4. Stir in the flour. salt. baking powder. and cocoa powder.

5. Set 2 cups of the batter aside.

6. Grease 13x9x2-inch pan.

7. Spread remaining batter in pan.

8. Evenly arrange the peppermint patties in a single layer over batter.

9. Spread the reserved 2 cups batter over the peppermint patties.

10. Bake at 350F for 50-55 minutes (until brownies begin to pull away from the sides of the pan).

11. Let cool in the pan on wire rack.

Content Warning: Anxiety, OCD, Depression

I was the kid who was too afraid to check out a library book, because what if I accidentally spilled something on it or heaven forbid, lose one?! I was also the kid who told my mother that I absolutely had to get perfect grades so I could be top of my class and get a scholarship to college, all when I was in 1st grade.

It was at the age of 10 that I stopped wanting to go to bed at night because I was terrified of dying in my sleep. How did I know this was a thing that could happen? I have no idea. (I'll blame the media.) This preoccupation only escalated as I lost 4 women who I loved very much, culminating with the death of my dearest grandmother when I was 15. My grandmother was one of my best friends and confidantes. When I stayed over at her house, we would stay up late to watch bad Lifetime movies and sneak York Peppermint Patties out of the freezer. After she passed, the fear was so intense, I would spend countless hours in the dark crying and listening to classical music while attempting to understand what would happen if I were to never wake up again.

By my "Sweet" 16 I had spiraled into a terrible clinical depression and began cycles of binge eating and then extreme calorie restriction to cope with the emotional trauma. I became obsessed with my appearance and counting. Counting calories, counting steps, counting ceiling tiles, counting whatever I could to take my mind off reality. Over the span of 4 years, I gained almost 50 pounds and hated myself.

With the support of my wonderful parents, I began to go to therapy. I was diagnosed with generalized anxiety disorder, obsessive compulsive disorder, and depression- diagnoses that actually made sense to me! Finally, I had some words to explain the chronic buzzing in my brain and the sadness in my heart.

I began a regimen of medication, therapy, and nutritional advice; however, there was still an emptiness within me. And then, I rediscovered dance. I joined a group on my college campus that welcomed dancers of all skill levels and styles. It felt amazing to get out of my head and back into my body and to use my body in an art of self-expression. I even started teaching my own hip hop class. (Thanks, Beyonce!) The confidence and happiness I gained from dancing permeated into my interpersonal relationships. I began to open up to my family and friends about what I was going through and as it turns out, the people who truly love you are really understanding and there are even other people out there who are solitarily suffering through their own problems. My joy for dance prompted me to seek out other joys: reading, writing poetry, acting, painting, and activism. Joy breeds joy!

Looking back, I wish I had talked sooner about what I was going through. And now, I can't talk about it enough. Gaining a voice about my mental health has given me the strength to speak up about other social justice issues, and I've allowed myself to be my fully nerdy, overly enthusiastic, pop-n-locking, perpetually anxious self.

BIO

Ally

Alexandra Elizabeth Sexton Thompson OD (Ally to her friends) is an eye doctor with a vision for a world without blindness and without mental health stigma. She grew up in Lincoln. RI. and now lives in Duxbury. MA. with her husband. Dave. and their cat. Tom. Ally has always had an enthusiasm for reading. writing. science. and education. She graduated valedictorian of her high school. first in her psychology program at Providence College. and she attended the New England College of Optometry to receive her doctorate. Ally enjoys hip hop dance. pairing chocolate with wine. true crime podcasts. exploring new cities. and all things nerdy. especially Harry Potter.

Notes, Thoughts & Goals

Michelle's Cheesecake

Ingredients:

Cheesecake Crust
- 2 cups graham cracker crumbs
- ½ cup granulated sugar
- 5 Tbsp. unsalted butter melted

Cheesecake
- 32 ounces cream cheese softened
- I and I/3 cups of granulated sugar
- I cup sour cream. room temperature
- I Tbsp. vanilla extract
- 4 large eggs. room temperature. lightly beaten

Notes to add my own voice to this recipe!

Cheesecake Crust

1. Move the oven rack to the lower third position and preheat the oven to 350°F.
2. Wrap the outer bottom of a 9-inch pan tightly with aluminum foil. Combine the graham cracker crumbs. sugar. and melted butter. Press the crumb mixture into the bottom and about 2-inches up the sides of the pan.
3. Bake for 10 minutes.
4. Set aside to cool while you make the filling.

Cheesecake

1. Reduce the oven temperature to 300°f degrees.
2. In a large mixing bowl. beat the cream cheese with an electric mixer until smooth and creamy. for about 1 minute.
3. Add the sugar and sour cream. beat until well combined.
4. Add the vanilla and beat on low speed until smooth. Gently stir in the eggs just until combined. Pour the batter over the prepared crust.
5. Fill a roasting pan with a few inches of boiling water and place the cheesecake in the center.
6. Bake for 1 hour. or until the edges are set and the center is slightly jiggly.
7. Turn the oven off and leave the cheesecake in the water bath in the oven for another hour. Remove the cheesecake from the water bath and place it on a wire rack. Run a small knife around the outer edge of the cheesecake to loosen it from the pan and leave it to cool completely. Cover and refrigerate for at least 4 hours. preferably overnight.
8. Remove the sides of the pan just before serving.

Content Warning: Addiction

Michelle S.
Clean Date: December 26, 2000

At this point, recovery for me is about everything: including material addiction not just alcohol or drugs. It means beginning with a foundation of innocence, getting back to who I was as a kid and the innate wisdom that goes along with that unscathed personality. Without these traits. one may remain abstinent from drugs and alcohol, but may never be truly satisfied. They may move from partner to partner, amassing material items only to be left feeling empty and dissatisfied.

My main motivation in being on the is earth, at this point in my short journey, is in spirituality. It's the main course of which I want to grow. I have some desires and I have some wants of course for the material, but I do not angle my life that way and surprisingly, I'm well taken care of.

I don't take any great pride in the fact that I have not used alcohol or drugs since Dec. 2000. I just don't want to put anything in me that clouds my vision, inhibits my spirituality or stunts my inner and outer growth. I reached for alcohol and drugs at a college age because it was simply "fun". I wasn't depressed, anxious or in desperate need of a social life. That fun path took me to pretty dark places. I sort of had a feeling I'd get addicted when I started using hard drugs but I was also really curious what addiction felt like. I wasn't quite satisfied in general with what this adult life was.

I used drugs hard for about 8 or 9 years, heroin and crystal meth mainly but in the end, heroin was the "go to". The last 3 years or so included drug treatment programs like detoxes and halfway houses. I was homeless in San Francisco off and on for the last three years of using; which was mainly what motivated me to start the treatment process.

When I say homeless - I'm not talking about couch surfing, I'm talking about wandering the streets every night looking for a place to safely close my eyes for a minute. It gave me great skills: resourceful skills that I can use today. I learned to sleep anywhere... although over the past 18 years, I have grown to enjoy a stable roof and a warm bed, I know I can still sleep anywhere.

I'm motivated today at this moment to look at myself, and really witness myself. See where I go wrong, why I feel the way I do at times. What earthly things am I attached or attracted to and why? I am motivated today to take care of my emotional, spiritual and physical well-being. I'm not sure 100% why but at some point, in my early recovery from addiction I realized I like feeling "well" in all aspects of the word.

I start my day (whether I feel like it or not) meditating. I sit for anywhere from 5 minutes to an hour depending what I'm feeling and make a conscious effort to connect with my heart and connect that heart to the Divine power that exists all around me. I make an attempt to surrender to that power and leave the heavy stuff up to God. I then usually go for a run outdoors. I found that running and meditation combined leads me to a pretty balanced personality. Overdoing either does the opposite.

I'm not anything special by any means, however since I work in the counseling field, I am really curious to know what qualities are within me that keep me motivated to do these things even if I'm not feeling great. I would love to be able to pass these qualities on to others knowing that sometimes people I meet cannot just get themselves to do it. Is it because I tried and felt better so I'm motivated to go on? Is it my upbringing? My genetics? Don't get me wrong I'm still such a work in progress. In quoting recovery terms "more will be revealed".

BIO

Michelle S.

As a clinician and person in recovery. Michelle has the privilege of seeing both sides of the story. Acquiring a master's degree in 2016 at the young age of 44. Michelle has also incorporated a career in education at the local community college. Michelle volunteers as a meditation instructor for a group called Sahaja Yoga Meditation. at a local community room in downtown Salem. MA. This meditation. Michelle says. is what lays the foundation of her entire life. Sahaja Yoga Meditation has given her a life purpose. a group of friends from all over the world. and a solid understanding of who she is and why she is on this planet.

Notes, Thoughts & Goals

Kayla's Healthy Banana Bread

Ingredients:

- 1 3/4 cups whole wheat flour
- ½ tsp. ground cinnamon
- 1 tsp. baking soda
- ½ tsp. salt
- 2 eggs
- ½ cup coconut oil. melted
- 1/3 cup honey
- 1/4 cup Greek Yogurt
- 1 tsp. vanilla extract
- 1 cup mashed ripe bananas (2-3 medium bananas)
- ½ cup dark chocolate chips. walnuts or raisins (optional)

Notes to add my own voice to this recipe!

Directions

1. Preheat the oven to 325f degrees. Grease a loaf pan and set aside.

2. In a medium bowl. whisk the flour. cinnamon. baking soda and salt. Set aside.

3. In a large bowl. beat the eggs. oil. honey. yogurt. and vanilla for 2 minutes. Stir in the bananas.

4. Mix in the dry ingredients.

5. Optional: stir in the dark chocolate chips. walnuts or raisins.

6. Pour batter into the greased loaf pan. sprinkle with some more cinnamon. raw sugar. or banana slices (optional)

7. Bake for 10-13 minutes

To make this vegan: use almond milk. flax eggs and maple syrup

Content Warning: Eating Disorder

I composed these poems during the early stages of my treatment, a very difficult time in my recovery. Poetry was my way of coping with the complexities my eating disorder presented. I hope this art will give you some insight into what it is like dealing with an eating disorder in all its intricacy.

Naked

Standing there clad in skin,
An eerie sense of bareness
Creeping up the small of my back,
Sprouting goose bumps of insecurity.
My artful hands begin to mold my body
Turning it into a perfect creation.
There is nothing flawed about its texture or build,
Just a weightless object.
Social and self acceptance gravitate towards it,
It is a leader and a role model,
Exhibiting health, beauty, and pride
Aesthetically pleasing to the eye
But a sudden environmental change creates
A lost sensation of power,
A sunken feeling of loneliness.
The world becomes an evil eye watching me closely,
Criticizing and analyzing my uniqueness
To feed its mind.
My body begins to itch and disintegrate,
Naked and attuned to the feelings exercise and appearance mask
Naked and no longer driven by the world's requests
Naked and loved by my body
Naked and proud to be me.

VI.

Is this my life or is it merely a façade?
A figment of my demented imagination,
A search for radical acceptance and control
To collect the particles of disappointment
And scatter them about the earth
Seeds giving birth to dreams,
Buds giving birth to opportunity,
Flowers giving birth to freedom
A garden of misfortune and greatness
I am the planter,
The creator,
The life giver
Helpless and lost
In the roots of my mind
A maze of mirrors each reflecting onto the next
A distorted image of reality
A victim of the world's witchcraft.
Now I am hidden and lifeless,
Soon I will be better
Soon I will be me.

IX.

Numbers define my life.
As I determine my self-worth based upon their value
I construct a world of fear and critical observation,
Which I am ready to obstruct
Though it will be challenging and uncomfortable
I know I am worthy of this beautiful, healthy life that I idolize
It is free from restriction and rigidity,
Connected to love and passion
The road to this place is blind
The unknown will soon become known
And the feeling will pass, my body will get through
I will find my purpose,
Practice my talents and sharpen my mind
I am a woman who has suffered and who will persevere
Who will look beyond the subjective and fight to subdue the
unnecessary voices

XI.

Let us just let go
Leave fate to its own devices
Allow trust to persevere
I have the power
I can overcome this
Let us just let go
And watch the journey rather than narrate it
Learn to love the indescribable
Conquer the fears and worries
Believe in this process
What is it that I must leave behind?
The stronghold that overpowers me
The torture I pursue
Let us just let go

XIII.

I do not want to do this, but I know I need to.
It is draining the life out of me,
Pouring out nothing but sadness.
Voices
Haunting me, telling me what is right and what is wrong
Voices
Some singing, some yelling, some merely whispering.
Sounds of truth, murmurs of falsity,
Invading my castle of innocence.
"Dig down deep" they say
To find my motivation, my purpose,
But it is too easy to avoid such work
And comply with the comfortable, the safe
Seeking only what is known
And trusting only what is visible.
But I mustn't
I mustn't
I must challenge those feelings,
Those thoughts,
Transform the anger into acceptance,
The depression into delight,
And the frustration into freedom.

XIV.

A life of curiosity,
Full of laughter and lust
Rhythm in movement and being
A healthy balance between mind and body,
Accessing my inner self
And no longer allowing it to simmer in my soul
Awaiting a wake-up call.
Happiness and hope transform the body,
Making it more beautiful and complete with pleasure,
Acceptance of the "had beens" and elimination of the
"should haves,"
No longer a fear of the unknown,
But rather a welcoming of that which the future holds
Recreating a life worthy of my love and dedication.

BIO

Kayla Yates

Kayla is an artist, a dancer, a poet, and a scientist. She believes that arts and humanities can enhance healthcare by transcending boundaries and fostering creativity. She plans to further explore the intersection of artistry and clinical competency to promote the accessibility and advancement of medicine Kayla enjoys traveling, exploring the outdoors, and drinking a hot cup of coffee in the morning. Through movement, she explores and connects with her environment. She is intrigued by the mechanics of the body, eager to learn more and apply her knowledge and skill to promote wellness. Her motivation for pursuing a career in the healthcare field stems from a deep understanding that relationships empower and heal the mind and the body. Her goal is to help people optimize their health, and to be a conduit for healing.

Nicole's Cookie Dough Cupcakes

Ingredients:

<u>Cookie Dough (make and freeze the night before)</u>
- 1 cup unsalted butter (room temperature)
- 3/4 cup granulated sugar
- 3/4 cup brown sugar
- 2 Tbsp. milk
- 1 Tbsp. vanilla
- 2 1/4 cups all-purpose flour
- 1/4 tsp. salt
- 3/4 cup mini chocolate chips

Cake Ingredients
- 1/2 cup unsalted butter
- 1 1/4 cups brown sugar
- 4 eggs (room temperature)
- 2 1/2 cups all-purpose flour
- 1/2 tsp. baking soda
- 1 tsp. baking powder
- 1 tsp. salt
- 1 cup whole milk
- 2 Tbsp. butter flavoring

Frosting Ingredients
- 1 cup unsalted butter
- 1/2 cup brown sugar
- 4 cups powdered sugar

Nicole's Cookie Dough Cupcakes

Ingredients:

Frosting Ingredients (cont.)
- 1/2 tsp. salt
- 2 Tbsp. milk
- 1 tsp. vanilla extract

Top with: mini chocolate chip cookies

Notes to add my own voice to this recipe!

Directions

Cookie Dough
1. Mix butter and sugars in mixing bowl until light and fluffy. for about 2 mins.
2. Beat in the milk and vanilla
3. Whisk the flour and salt together in a separate bowl. then add to batter until combined.
4. Stir in the chocolate chips.
5. Shape the dough into small balls and freeze on parchment paper overnight.

Cupcakes
1. Preheat the oven to 350 degrees.
2. Combine the butter and brown sugar in mixing bowl.
3. Add the eggs one at a time. beating after each egg.
4. Add room temperature eggs one at a time. beating after each egg.
5. In a separate bowl combine flour. baking soda. baking powder. and salt. Add the dry ingredients to mixing bowl. alternating with the milk. Blend in the butter flavoring.
6. Fill 20 lined muffin cups 2/3 full (use 4 tablespoon scoop). Place a frozen cookie dough ball into each muffin cup. then bake for 17-18 minutes.

Frosting
1. Combine the butter and brown sugar in a mixing bowl on medium speed until light and fluffy.
2. Beat in the powdered sugar 1 cup at a time.
3. Beat in the salt. milk and vanilla until combined and smooth.
4. Frost each cupcake with the mixture.
5. After frosting. add the mini chocolate chip cookies.

Content Warning: Depression, Anxiety

I believe I have been fighting depression and anxiety since my early teen years. However, it was during the last six years of my life, that things got much worse. I would sit at home with my thoughts swirling in my head, most of which revolved around how horrible I was. Speaking on the phone and going to public places scared me immensely. I often asked my ever-supportive husband to do things for me. When my friends asked me to go somewhere, I found an excuse not to participate, even though deep down, I craved connection. My anxiety got to the point where just thinking about going out, made me physically sick.

In the beginning of 2015, I got tired of feeling so awful and I forced myself to go to the doctor. The doctor prescribed me an anti-anxiety medication, but it was during this time, we discovered that I had depression too. It got to the point where I would hide in my bedroom and refuse to let anyone in. I had suicidal thoughts and was embarrassed about my feelings; I hated myself on so many levels.

In the summer of 2015, everything started to change. My 11-year-old daughter and I took a cake decorating class online. It helped us bond, and a few months later we started a cupcake business out of our home. Although I was still nervous about going to social events, we started attending "Food Truck Friday" events and boutique stores to sell our cupcakes. We met so many people as a result and the more I got to know them, the more I realized: I was not alone in my struggles. We also recognized that we could use our cupcakes to help others and started donating them as often as we could. In September 2017, we started "Project Kindness". This project gave us the opportunity to surprise a person or local business, who was struggling. We would bring them cupcakes, fudge and other small donated gifts.

When we started the project, I would ask my family to come with me on our deliveries, but I eventually got to the point where I was able to do some of them all by myself, a huge breakthrough!

Fast forward to March 2018, I found out that my family would be moving from Utah to Massachusetts, a place I had never even visited. I have always cried easily, but when hearing this news, I cried for weeks. When we got to Massachusetts, my family and I stayed in a hotel for three weeks until we could move into our new home. During that time, I did nothing but watch TV and eat junk food. I knew I had the support of my family and friends in Utah, but I just didn't want to be here anymore. A couple of months later though, we got settled into our new house, and after a lot of hard work, I was able to start my cupcake business up again. Our new community has been incredibly welcoming and I am feeling much better. I still have days where it is hard to get out of bed, but the days I bake and share acts of kindness, I am in my happy place...and that is certainly worth fighting for!

BIO

Nicole Mitchell

Nicole, affectionately nicknamed "The Cupcake Lady" by her friends, learned from her mother at a young age how to bake. When Nicole's daughter, Kalista, was 11 years old, they also bonded over baking and opened a small cupcake shop out of their home in Stansbury Park, UT. Because Nicole loves to help others, she quickly made kindness the focus of the business and changed the name to "Kind Hearts and Cupcakes." Nicole currently lives in Sagamore Beach, MA, where she reopened her home bakery. The organization's mission revolves around volunteering and donating to charity events. Her business thrives on surprising people with treats and small gifts, fostering love through baking.

Kristen's Peanut Butter Oat Bites

Ingredients:

- 2 bananas
- 1 cup oats
- 2 Tbsp. powdered peanut butter (such as PB2)
- 1/4 cup chocolate chips

Notes to add my own voice to this recipe!

Directions

1. Preheat the oven to 350f degrees.
2. Mash up the bananas until they are smooth.
3. Add the oats. powdered peanut butter. and chocolate chips into the banana mixture.
4. Divide the mixture into small balls.
5. Place the balls on a greased cookie sheet.
6. Cook for 11-13 minutes.

My Story

I grew up the third of four daughters in my family. As an on-looker, it may have seemed as though my family had it all to-gether. We went to Disney nearly every year, and my mom stayed home with us kids and volunteered in our classrooms while my dad went off to work. Throughout my childhood, I was always considered the "tough" kid, playing sports year-round while also juggling academics, a social life, and an unpredictable home life. Sometimes I felt like I had no other choice but to be tough. I acted tough for my little sister, whom I adore, and for my parents, who spent a lot of their energy and resources on one of my older sisters, who was di-agnosed with Bipolar Disorder at a young age. I went through my childhood unknowingly being a people pleaser, making sure everyone around me was ok, even if I was not.

This continued through high school and college, and for about a year post-college graduation. I was living in Boston after college, and feeling on top of the world with a good job and better friends. It was back in March of 2017 that something changed in me, leaving me anxiety-ridden day in and day out. I could barely get out of bed to go to work and would wake up in the middle of the night in cold sweats and near tears. I realized that I had spent years of my life making sure everyone around me was ok, while I myself was not. I was conditioned to be tough from such a young age, and these feelings that I was having were so out of the ordinary. I ignorantly thought that being tough meant bottling your emotions up inside, and that therapy was for the weak. These thoughts couldn't be further from the truth.

About halfway through April of 2017, my mom graciously sat me down and coached me on how to find a therapist near me that would suit my needs. The first few sessions were unexplainably tough, for lack of a better term, but as time went on, I realized I was tough too... just not in the same way I had known the word as a child. Talking through things that you've bottled up for years requires strength and courage, and I'm happy to say that therapy has helped me grow more than I could ever have imagined. My therapist has helped me realize what is important to me - living a healthier lifestyle - and what's not so important to me anymore - going out and drinking excessively every weekend just because everyone else wants to, even when I don't. I now realize that going grocery shopping and making homemade banana bread on a Friday night is 100% ok for a 24-year-old, although not the "norm." It makes me feel ok and that's what matters.

I've learned so much about myself and my own mental health over the past year, and with a good therapist and close family and friends constantly supporting me, even at my worst, I can look back and see how far I've come. I wish I could tell myself a year and a half ago what I know now: it will not last forever, and you will get through this. Every day is a chance to keep working on myself and putting myself first. Some days are just plain awesome, while others not so much, but now with the right coping mechanisms that work for me, I can confidently remind myself, "This too shall pass," and I wholeheartedly believe it.

BIO

Kristen Sullivan

Kristen is a young professional working in the insurance industry. She loves to work out, try and share new recipes, and spend time with her family, friends, and boyfriend. She hopes to one day be a certified personal trainer and have an at-home fitness studio!

Notes, Thoughts & Goals

Suzanne's Chocolate Peanut Butter Swirl Cheesecake

Ingredients:

- 2 cups graham cracker crumbs
- 6 Tbsp. unsalted butter
- 1 ½ cups sugar
- 8 oz. semisweet chocolate
- 32 oz. cream cheese, softened
- ¼ cup milk
- 5 large eggs
- 2/3 cup creamy peanut butter

Notes to add my own voice to this recipe!

Directions

1. Preheat the oven to 475F degrees.

2. In a small bowl, mix graham cracker crumbs, butter, and ¼ cup of sugar. Press the mixture into a 10x3-inch springform pan, pressing it into the bottom and up the sides of the pan.

3. Refrigerate.

4. In a small saucepan over low heat, heat the chocolate until melted and smooth, stirring frequently. Remove the saucepan from the heat and cool the chocolate slightly.

5. In a large bowl, with a mixer at medium speed, beat the cream cheese until smooth. Then slowly beat in 1 ¼ cups of sugar. With the mixer at low speed, beat in the milk and eggs. Beat for 3 minutes, occasionally scraping the bowl with a rubber spatula.

6. Remove 1 cup of the batter to a small bowl. Stir the peanut butter into the small bowl until well blended.

7. With the remaining batter in the large bowl, add in the melted chocolate and blend, using the mixer at low speed. Pour the chocolate batter into the pan.

8. Spoon dollops of the peanut butter mixture into the batter in the pan.

9. With a knife, cut and twist the peanut butter through the mixture to obtain a marbled effect.

10. Bake the cheesecake for 10 minutes, then turn the oven to 300F degrees and bake for an additional 50 minutes.

Directions

11. Then turn the oven off.

12. Leave the cheesecake in the oven for 30 minutes longer. keeping the oven door slightly open.

13. Remove the cheesecake from the oven. Cool in the pan on a wire rack. Cover and refrigerate the cheesecake for at least 4 hours. or overnight. before removing from the springform pan.

Content Warning: Bipolar Disorder

When I was in my late teens, I was prescribed an antidepressant. Little did I know that taking that medication would lead me into the first of many manic episodes. By the time I reached my early 20s, I couldn't stay out of psychiatric hospitals because of my bipolar disorder. My episodes included staying up for days at a time, doing things in a frantic or all-consuming way, excessive drinking, dangerously promiscuous behavior, getting into debt, and more. All of this threw me into the depths of the deepest, darkest, soul-swallowing depression that insisted I end my life. All of this made me feel so sick, like the world was just too much for me.

Although I was living in the throes of my mental illness, one thing I made sure that I did consistently was seek help. With the support of my family, my therapist, my psychiatrist, and the hospital programs, I made progress. Throughout this journey, I made sure that I fought. Whether it was at the end of a therapy session or time in a hospital program, I fought. I fought to understand my illness, I fought to learn coping skills, and I fought to put one foot in front of the other - even when my mind, body, and soul were telling me to give up. I worked with my psychiatrist to find the right balance of medications to keep me out of the depressed place, but also out of the manic episodes. Though trying different medications took a lot of effort, I was persistent and never gave up. This is also when I learned how to ask for help and find support from family and friends. I also learned to look to myself for compassion and support.

It has been such a long road - one that I am still on. Most of the time, though, I don't feel sick or damaged. In fact, I feel like I am a productive member of society: strong and well.

Through treatment, I have come to feel like a different person and much more than my mental illness, but I do still struggle. Just a few months ago, I had a manic episode on my way to work; I started having visual hallucinations. Instead of telling myself that I was too sick or damaged to ask for help, I immediately went to my support system. I reached out to my doctor to get guidance on my medication. I also kicked into self-care mode and took some time off work, ensuring I got the rest that would help my symptoms. This was a scary time, but by reaching out and taking care of myself, I could get back on track quickly.

For me, I have learned what I need to take care of my mental illness daily. I have also learned that when I do just that, I can live an amazing life - one that is full of stability, structure, flexibility, connection, purpose, and love. That is the life I have today.

From a little girl who once believed that her all-consuming thoughts would eventually end her, being here today is a true miracle.

BIO

Suzanne Garveich

Suzanne is a 44-year-old woman who is happily married to her wife, Nikki DeRome. She has worked in Public Health Research over the last 20 years and holds her Master's Degree in Public Health from Northeastern University. Suzanne lives with Biploar II, anxiety, PTSD, and alcoholism. She is a survivor and is dedicated to fighting for her own mental wellness as well as breaking down barriers that exist for others. Her piece in this book is dedicated to her mother who passed away, and who showed her the joy of cooking, how to be a survivor, and unconditional love.

Shoshana's Oreo Truffles

Ingredients:

- 1 (16 oz.) package Oreo Sandwich Cookies
- 8 oz. cream cheese, softened
- 16 oz. semi-sweet baking chocolate, melted

Directions

1. Crush the Oreo cookies into fine crumbs. either in food processor or with rolling pin. and place them in a resealable plastic bag.

2. Add the cream cheese and mix well until blended.

3. Roll the cookie and cream cheese mixture into balls 1 inch in diameter.

4. In a small bowl. microwave and melt the semi-sweet baking chocolate.

5. Dip the Oreo and cream cheese balls into the melted chocolate. and line on wax paper.

6. Refrigerate until firm. about 1 hour.

Content Warning: Anxiety, Depression

Dear Reader,

My first year of college was the most challenging year of my life, but it led to necessary change. As I was gearing up for the move to college, I was scared to move out of my parents' house and into a dorm with strangers. I was concerned that I would not be smart enough to keep up with the challenging academics, and I was unsure that I would be popular enough to make friends. What I didn't realize was that my biggest issue in college was one I brought with me: my underlying depression and anxiety.

In my first months of college, I spent much of the time alone in my room and longing for familiarity. I struggled to socialize with others, and found each day was filled with more despair than the last. In hindsight, I realize the feelings I dismissed and attributed to an adjustment period were a new manifestation of an old problem.

By winter break, I decided I was ready for a change. Although I did not want to return to school in the spring, I entered the semester with hope because I had a plan to find more happiness in my life with the support of a therapist. Weekly phone calls with my therapist, discussing strategies for feeling better about my situation, felt tedious at times yet gave me the boost to make it through each week. Despite feeling discouraged and unmotivated, I persevered and spent the month applying to transfer to another college.

On the final night of my freshman year, I received a phone call from my top choice transfer school - I had been accepted for the fall! I celebrated that night by studying for my last final, then took the test the next morning. As I exited the exam room, I ceremoniously threw out my student ID card and exhaled a sigh of relief that I would never return to such a dark place: the place in my mind that kept me from feeling happy.

While I wish that I sought treatment sooner, I am proud to say that I have made it through one of the toughest times of my life and gained skills to cope with my mental illness. I hope my story helps others realize that while it is normal for us to go through difficult periods, we can't accept being miserable as the only option. While I still struggle with feelings of depression and anxiety and work through my problems in therapy, I promise myself that I can make decisions in my life that help me to never return to that dark place again.

BIO

Shoshana Fishbein

Shoshana is a public health enthusiast who is passionate about health promotion and education. She loves discussing evidence-based mental and physical health practices, napping, and red velvet cake with cream cheese frosting. She hopes that this book helps people everywhere know that mental health issues do not have to define their life, and that they can be treated.

Notes, Thoughts & Goals

Ariele's Lemon Loaf

Ingredients:

Lemon Loaf
- 1 ½ cups flour
- ½ tsp. baking powder
- ½ tsp. baking soda
- ½ tsp. salt
- 3 eggs. room temperature
- 1 cup sugar
- 2 Tbsp. butter. softened
- 1 tsp. vanilla extract
- 2 tsp. lemon extract
- 1/3 cup lemon juice
- ½ cup oil
- zest of one lemon

Glaze
- 1 cup powdered sugar
- 2 Tbsp. whole milk
- ½ tsp. lemon extract

Notes to add my own voice to this recipe!

Directions

1. Preheat oven to 350F degrees. Grease and flour a 9x5-inch loaf pan.

2. In a large bowl. combine the flour. baking powder. baking soda. and salt.

3. In a medium bowl. combine the eggs. sugar. butter. vanilla extract. lemon extract. and lemon juice with a mixer until blended.

4. Pour the wet ingredients into the dry ingredients and blend until smooth.

5. Add the oil and lemon zest and mix well.

6. Pour into the loaf pan. and bake for 45 minutes until a toothpick comes out clean. Remove from the oven and cool on a rack.

7. In a medium bowl. combine the glaze ingredients. Whisk the ingredients together until blended. Then spread the glaze evenly over the cooled loaf.

Content Warning: Addiction

My name is Ariele Goldman, and my life is beautiful. I am 30 years old and reside in Salem, MA. I'm a dog mom, a daughter, a fiancé and a friend. I work for an amazing company where I get to help people better their lives every day. I'm a student and an intern. There is another part of me, a very important part: I am a recovering addict. My life didn't always consist of love, hope, hard work, and learning; It was once dark and horrific.

I would definitely say that I was born with the disease of addiction. A powerful force inside my soul constantly needed to be fed by outside things to make me feel better. From as far back as I can remember, my inner voice screamed at me "I am not good enough," "I am worthless," "No one loves me".... and I believed it all...as if these phrases were simple facts, like an apple is fruit.

While all of this occurred internally, externally my childhood was wonderful. I had two loving parents, a beautiful home to live in, plenty of food to eat, and the list goes on. All of the cards I was dealt in life could have led me to succeed, but none of that mattered. My addictions and obsessions started with small and innocent things: beanie babies, Pokémon cards, pogs. As I got older and my internal pain and self-hatred got worse, so did my addictions and my demons. I turned to food for comfort. I gained a lot of weight and struggled with an eating disorder. I latched on to people, in a codependent manner, to validate me in ways I could not validate myself. Eventually, the ways in which I tried to make myself feel better no longer worked.

It was in high school that I first tried alcohol. It was the first time I was finally able to quiet that nasty inner voice. I had fun. I finally felt like I fit in. I could laugh, be silly, let loose, and not have my mind running a mile a minute. Little did I know my solution to feeling better at the time was the beginning of the end. Just like before, this temporary fix no longer worked and my disease progressed to the depths of hell, swallowing me whole. In time, I became an IV drug user. I lost everything that ever mattered to me. The drugs took my soul. They took EVERYTHING.

I am so thankful that I got to that point where I was so broken, so lost, and so desperate to find a new way to live that I got help. I found that I wasn't alone. I found that there were other people like me who had been where I had been and had found a solution. I have been clean and sober since January 24th, 2017.

I'm grateful for everything I have been through in my life, because it has made me the strong woman I am today.

Lindsay's Peanut Butter Blossom Cookies

Ingredients:

- 1 cup brown sugar
- 1 cup unsalted butter, softened
- 1 cup peanut butter
- 2 eggs
- ¼ cup milk
- 2 tsp. vanilla
- 3 ½ cups flour
- 2 tsp. baking soda
- 1 tsp. salt
- approx. ½ cup white sugar
- 1 (12 oz.) bag Hershey's kisses (unwrapped)

Notes to add my own voice to this recipe!

Directions

1. Preheat the oven to 350f degrees.

2. In a large bowl. combine the brown sugar. butter. and peanut butter with a mixer.

3. Add the eggs. milk. and vanilla. and mix again until fully incorporated

4. Sift together the flour. baking soda. and salt. Gradually add to the peanut butter mixture until well blended.

5. Shape the dough into 1-inch balls and roll in white sugar to coat.

6. Place on a baking sheet and bake for 8-12 minutes.

7. Remove from the oven and gently press one unwrapped Hershey kiss into each cookie.

8. Let cool before serving.

Content Warning: Anxiety

To those who struggle with their mental health:

You are not alone. Like most college students, during my first few years at Northeastern University I struggled with the stress surrounding academic performance, body image, relationships, and general fulfillment. This accumulation of anxiety finally broke me when I was an intern halfway around the world and my first serious relationship took a turn for the worse.

For months, I lived in a minor depressive state until I finally made the choice to go to therapy. Fortunately, this decision came earlier than it does for most – as a pre-medical/public health student, I had learned about the importance of mental health in many of my classes, and I knew that I could not let the stigma around the topic prevent me from getting the help I clearly needed. I talked to my parents and closest friends about my decision, and realized that I was silly not to ask for their support sooner. It took me about a year of weekly therapy sessions to fully take control of my anxiety, my decisions, and my life.

Even though I'm the happiest I have ever been, I continue to attend therapy sessions to this day! I personally believe that every single person, no matter what their situation is, could benefit from talking to a therapist, even if it's simply about general life decisions. I look back and can't believe how far I've come since I started college. If I can make the journey towards becoming a happy and fulfilled individual, then anyone can!

BIO

Lindsay Fisher

Lindsay Fisher is a young professional currently living and working in Boston. Originally from Norwich. CT. she recently graduated with her Master's Degree in Public Health from Northeastern University and is currently applying to medical school. Outside of her job as a research coordinator at Massachusetts General Hospital. her passion is triathlon. She is training to complete her first full Ironman distance triathlon in the summer of 2019. Her other hobbies include SoulCycle. cooking. and trying new restaurants.

Allison's Angel Food Cake

Ingredients:

Cake
- 1 ¾ cups sugar
- ¼ tsp. salt
- 1 cup cake flour
- 12 egg whites, room temperature
- ½ cup warm water
- 1 tsp. vanilla
- 1 ½ tsp. cream of tartar

Frosting
- 2 ¾ cups powdered sugar
- 6 Tbsp. unsweetened cocoa powder
- 6 Tbsp. unsalted butter
- 5 Tbsp. evaporated milk
- 1 tsp. vanilla extract

Notes to add my own voice to this recipe!

Directions

1. Preheat oven to 350f degrees.

2. Place the sugar in a food processor and blend for two minutes. until it be comes very fine.

3. In a small or medium bowl. combine the cake flour. salt. and half of the fine sugar. Sift together and set aside.

4. In a large bowl. combine the egg whites. water. vanilla. and cream of tartar. Whisk the ingredients together by hand for 2 minutes. until well combined. At this point. switch to a hand mixer. or pour the egg white mixture into the bowl of a stand mixer and use a whisk attachment. Gradually add the remaining half of the sugar. and beat the egg white mixture until medium peaks form.

5. Sprinkle some of the flour mixture over the top of the egg white mixture. Gently stir in. Repeat until all the flour mixture has been stirred in evenly.

6. Spoon the mixture into an ungreased tube pan. Bake for 35 minutes until the cake is golden brown in color and cooked through.

7. Invert the cake pan and cool upside down (with the cake remaining in the pan) until completely cooled.

8. Once cooled. remove from the pan. carefully scraping the edges to sepa rate them from the pan.

Directions

Frosting Directions

1. In a medium bowl, sift together the powdered sugar and cocoa, then set aside.

2. In a large bowl, cream the butter until smooth, then gradually beat in the sugar mixture alternating with the evaporated milk. Blend in the vanilla. Beat until light and fluffy. If necessary, adjust the consistency with more milk or sugar.

3. Once the cake has cooled, add the frosting.

Content Warning: OCD, Food rituals

Mental illnesses tend to be hard to identify, and mine was no exception. I'm diagnosed with Obsessive Compulsive Disorder (OCD), which for me manifested as an obsession with food and a compulsion to control it. This looks and sounds more like an eating disorder, which also helped obscure it. Disordered eating is insidiously shrouded and even rewarded in the world today. It was easy for me to hide from and justify my behavior, because of course it's a good thing to make healthy choices and be conscious of intake, right?

The criterion that turns a pattern of behaviors into a disorder is their degree of interference in daily life - plenty of people are conscious of their diet and become anxious when faced with food insecurity, but not everyone finds themselves obsessing over choosing restaurants, or staying home from social gatherings out of fear of what they might eat. It took me a long time to step back and realize that my tendencies had actually become barriers that kept me from being who I wanted to be.

I ended up in a fantastic type of therapy called Cognitive Behavioral Therapy (CBT) in which you catch, label, and analyze your thoughts for distortions. I basically had to label and rank my fears, then confront them one by one until they became less scary. That was some of the weirdest and hardest homework I've ever had to do - who else can say they've been assigned to eat an entire chocolate bar first thing in the morning?

My treatment and my recovery are centered around breaking the strict rules I have built around food. I'm still working hard at it, and I am improving every day. One of the best and most rewarding parts of the process for me is cooking! I love to lose myself in the cooking process - it's almost like meditation when you're focused. It's also harder to restrict or shy away from something I made myself, because if I spend time on a dish and am proud of it, I want to enjoy it! This has also become a great tool for me to push myself, and I've added back foods that I previously restricted by making something with them myself.

It's easy to rationalize a disorder and let it overstay its welcome as a crappy roommate in your brain, but that is no way to live, and we sometimes need a little help evicting that roommate. Therapy is one of the most impactful things I've ever done, and I cannot overstate how helpful it was for me. I truly believe it can help anyone!

BIO

Allison Powers

Allison is a student studying Economics and Psychology at Occidental College. She is expected to graduate in the spring of 2019. She hopes to work in research and return to school for data science. Allison has been involved with Active Minds, a mental health advocacy club, for the entirety of her college career, and will continue to be an advocate after graduation. In her free time, she enjoys being outdoors and playing with dogs.

Mallory's Gluten-Free Cake

Ingredients:

Cake
- 1 box gluten-free white or yellow cake mix or chocolate cake mix
- 8 oz. Greek yogurt
- 1 package vanilla instant pudding mix
- ¼ cup coconut oil or canola oil
- 4 eggs

Topping
- 2-3 tsp. cinnamon
- 1/3 cup sugar
- 1 package (12oz.) chocolate chips

Notes to add my own voice to this recipe!

Directions

1. Preheat the oven to 350f degrees.

2. In a large bowl. mix the cake mix. Greek yogurt. instant pudding. oil. and eggs.

3. In a separate bowl. mix together the cinnamon and sugar.

4. Grease a round cake pan.

5. Pour half of the batter into the cake pan.

6. Sprinkle half of the cinnamon and sugar mixture and half of the chocolate chips into the batter. and spread them evenly across the batter.

7. Pour in the rest of the batter.

8. Sprinkle on the remainder of the cinnamon and sugar mixture and the chocolate chips.

9. Bake in the oven for about 40-45 minutes.

10. Test with a toothpick to ensure it is cooked through. If not. return it to the oven until it is no longer runny.

11. Err on the side of under-baking ever so slightly. as gluten-free baked goods dry out if overbaked.

Content Warning: Depression and Anxiety

Mental health and gut health have become undeniably intertwined as more professionals have spoken out about the connection between the two. So it shouldn't have come as a surprise when my gut health took a turn for the worse after years of struggling with depression and anxiety. And while it's like asking whether the chicken or the egg came first, I am unsure which illness truly came first. What I do know is that whether the Irritable Bowel Syndrome or the mental illness came first felt irrelevant at the time. I was in significant pain, and I desperately needed to heal my ailing mind and body. When I was diagnosed with IBS, I often felt sick to my stomach, which fueled my anxiety. It became a daily battle to leave my apartment. Not leaving my apartment often forced me into isolation, which serves as a source of hope to the survival of depression. My worsening depression made it even more arduous to stomach any food, furthering my stomach woes. I felt trapped in the cycle of these three illnesses, a cycle that was sucking the life from my being. I knew I needed to make a change. That's when I made the decision to cut gluten from my diet. The fact that gluten can cause inflammation was a concept I had been vaguely familiar with, but I never wanted to go through the effort of consciously cutting out many of the foods I enjoyed. My body told a different tale: it was crying out in pain. I could no longer ignore its cries, so I gave the gluten-free diet a shot.

Becoming gluten free didn't solve all the issues I was faced with, but it certainly did bring about some much-needed relief. My stomach pain eased, allowing me to leave my apartment, enjoy the company of friends, and get back to the activities I had pulled away from. The more conscious I became of my gluten intake, the more empowered I felt in my journey in recovery. It gave me the ability to not just live but to be alive.

One thing this change didn't lend itself to was the consumption of baked goods. I cannot deny my love for some homemade goodies. I took it upon myself to reinvent recipes I had loved so dearly but was no longer able to eat. I didn't always want to be left out of the dessert course. That's when I took a coffee cake that had been baked into my childhood memories, and tinkered with it so that it would meet my dietary needs. The recipe I've shared features my tinkering come to fruition. Food makes a difference in how we feel, and treating yourself to something sweet doesn't have to come with painful consequences. Here's to finding the food that works for you! Happy eating!

BIO

Mallory Gothelf

Mallory Gothelf is a writer, speaker, mental health advocate, and her friends' designated baker. Having grown up with a mom who owned a baking business, she has been playing with batters and doughs for as long as she can remember. Struggling with Irritable Bowel Syndrome (IBS) and mental illness, baking became a great way to focus her attention on something other than her illnesses. Baking also allowed Mallory to recreate her favorite baked goods with alternative ingredients that comply with her restricted diet. This is surely the tastiest coping mechanism Mallory has in her toolbox.

Notes, Thoughts & Goals

Kara's Whole Wheat Pumpkin Chocolate Chip Zucchini Bread (yields 2 loaves)

Ingredients:

- 2 medium zucchini, shredded (about 3 cups)
- 1 cup coconut sugar
- 2/3 cup pumpkin puree
- 1/3 cup maple syrup
- 2 tsp. vanilla extract
- 4 eggs
- 3 cups white whole wheat flour
- 2 tsp. baking soda
- ½ tsp. baking powder
- 1 tsp. salt
- 1 tsp. cinnamon
- 1 cup walnut halves, chopped and divided
- ½ cup mini chocolate chips

Notes to add my own voice to this recipe!

Directions

1. Preheat the oven to 350F degrees. Grease two 9x5-inch loaf pans with butter or cooking spray.

2. In a large bowl, mix together the zucchini, coconut sugar, pumpkin, maple syrup, vanilla, and eggs.

3. In a medium bowl, whisk together the flour, baking soda, baking powder, salt, and cinnamon until combined.

4. Stir the dry ingredients into the wet until combined. Fold in the chocolate chips and walnuts, reserving about ¼ cup of walnuts for the topping.

5. Divide the batter evenly into both pans. Bake 70-80 minutes, or until a toothpick inserted into the center comes out clean. Cool in the pans for 10 minutes before removing the loaves from the pans and cooling on a rack. Cool the bread completely before serving.

My Story

A few years ago, I wasn't owning my story. When people would ask me how I got into the nutrition field, I'd tell them I became a vegetarian at a young age and that as a result I had to learn about nutrition and how to make sure I was nourishing my body as a pre-teen vegetarian. And all of that is true – it's not like I've been lying to everyone, but that version is the short, safe one. Not the entire story.

So why was I hesitant to spill it all? Well, it all stems back to when I was a senior in college, majoring in nutrition and getting ready to apply for my dietetic internship (a DI is the clinical experience required to become a registered dietitian nutritionist). We had some kind of DI fair where all the local DI directors came to talk about their programs, and there were a couple lectures about the application process, essay writing, etc. And one thing they said hit me like a ton of bricks, and I could feel the shame rising in me.

"If you have an eating disorder or have had an eating disorder in the past, do not talk about it in your essay or application – you will not get matched if you do. And you should reconsider going into this field, too – you won't be an effective counselor..."

I stopped listening. I felt a pit in the bottom of my stomach. I started sweating. I felt so.much.shame. And in that moment, I decided I would bury the story of my eating disorder so that I could become a dietician.

And the short, safe story lived on.

Until a year ago...

I've read a lot of Brené Brown over the last few years, and she talks a lot about shame and owning your own story. And she says that in order to combat shame, you have to speak about it. The more you harbor it inside, the more it grows and takes over.

I was done harboring my shame and hiding behind my true story. When I was writing my e-book, Nourish Your Namaste, this time last year, I decided I was ready to own my story about how nutrition and yoga saved me. To tell the whole story. The one that's imperfect and real and beautiful. The one that's authentically me.

And yes, it involved an eating disorder.

Growing up, I was always the shortest kid in my class. If I had a class to be in today, chances are I'd still be the shortest. And so when I put on some weight when I was ten years old (pre-puberty), I was subjected to ridicule in school. Because now I was short and fat. Girls were cruel. Like really cruel. Like whispering behind my back that they wanted to push me off a cliff cruel. Many days I came home crying. And so that's when I saw my first nutritionist. I don't remember much of what we talked about in that appointment besides popcorn. Yes, I could still eat popcorn. It was on the "approved" snacks list. I loved popcorn. Phew. But what I do remember is that at no time did any healthcare professional tell me or my parents that putting on some weight pre-puberty is NORMAL and nothing to be concerned about.

A few years later, more overheard comments about my weight from family and friends, a new best friend with an eating disorder, a big life change over which I had no control, and my own eating disorder was formed. I restricted my food intake. I lost weight. Too much weight. I stopped getting my period. This lasted about a year or so until one day I re-

-member panicking, "Wait, am I not going to be able to have kids someday?"

And so back to a dietician I went. This time because I was underweight.

I remember crying in her office. Feeling out of control once again. Thinking that the amount of food she wanted me to eat sounded insane. I felt defeated.

Luckily, the treatment coincided with me going to high school with a new group of friends, all of whom had very healthy relationships with food. I slowly started to heal, to eat what I wanted to eat without guilt, to mend my relationship with food, to rediscover satisfaction from food, to put the weight back on, and to restore my period.

And so, all of this backstory is to say that THIS is the real reason I went into nutrition. I wanted to help girls like me who struggled with eating disorders and their relationships with food.

It wasn't until I started my own business that I started to re-connect with my original passion for the field. I started counseling clients again and learned about the work of intuitive eating. And all a sudden everything felt like it began to click. I started to feel fulfilled in my work again. Like soul-warming, ultra-gratifying fulfilled.

I wouldn't wish an eating disorder upon anyone. I wouldn't wish it upon my younger self. But since I did go through it, I'm glad that I was able to take the darkness and turn it into light. I'm glad that my suffering ultimately led me to help others who are suffering.

BIO

Kara Lydon

Kara Lydon. RD. LDN. RYT. The Foodie Dietitian. is a nationally recognized and award-winning registered dietitian nutritionist. certified intuitive eating counselor. and yoga teacher. Kara believes that the key to authentic health and well-being is celebrating food and our bodies. and she instills this positive philosophy in the kitchen. yoga studio. working one-on-one with clients. and in her food. It also permeates her healthy living blog. The Foodie Dietitian. and her e-book. Nourish Your Namaste: How Nutrition and Yoga Can Support Digestion. Immunity. Energy and Relaxation. Her blog features delicious. nourishing seasonal recipes and simple strategies to bring more yoga and mindfulness into your life. and has been featured in countless national online publications. When she's not working. Kara loves going for nature walks and hikes. trying new restaurants. traveling. and spending time at home in Boston. MA. with her husband and her furry cat. Constantine.

What is self-care?

Self-care is any act done purposefully to enhance or sustain your mental or physical wellness. There are several ways to practice self-care. Entertainment media often portrays self-care as "bubble baths and lattes," but experts suggest that self-care can be as simple or mundane as paying bills or doing laundry, if it is an intentional practice to better one's health.

Self-care is personal, and one must find the right activities and balance that feel best for oneself. Sometimes this takes trial and error, so below are several suggestions that you can experiment with and hopefully incorporate.

Disclaimer: Self-care is incredibly important for anyone and everyone, but it is not a replacement for professional counseling, therapy, or medication management. Self-care can certainly compliment the work one is doing with a healthcare provider or on one's own, but it is important to remember that for some people, self-care is only part of the picture.

Finally, practice self-care without judgement! There is no "right" way to practice.

Ideas
Make and keep appointments: therapy, doctor, dentist, acupuncture, etc.
Go to bed early or take a nap.
Reach out to a friend: by email, text message, phone, or even snail mail.
Cook or bake something special.
Get a massage.
Take a shower or bath.
Say "no" to something.
Get a manicure or pedicure OR give yourself one.
Go outside.
Exercise for the sole purpose of improving your mood.
Unfollow toxic people on social media.
"Re-shop" or organize your closet.
Learn and use grounding techniques like deep breathing or mindfulness.
Read or listen to a book or podcast.
Purchase a coloring book and color.
Learn something new.
"Unplug" by avoiding use of your phone or computer for an established timeframe.
Listen to music, create a playlist, or make music if you play an instrument.
Make your bed.
Journal.
Enjoy a "good cry."
Make a gratitude list without judgement or any other expectations or guilt.
Name and observe emotions, but otherwise do not attach to them.
Meditate, or listen to a guided meditation.
Give back! Volunteer or participate in a community service activity.
Stretch.
Hydrate.
Take yourself out to dinner, a movie, or the theatre.

Part 3

The Art of Baking

Becca's Healthy Muffins

Ingredients:

- 1½ cups whole wheat flour
- ¾ cup ground flax seeds
- ¾ cup oatmeal
- 1 cup brown sugar
- 2 tsp. baking soda
- 1 tsp. baking powder
- ½ tsp. salt
- 2 tsp. cinnamon
- 1 cup shredded carrots
- 1 cup apples, peeled and finely chopped
- ½ cup raisins (or craisins)
- ¾ cup milk
- 2 eggs
- 1 tsp. vanilla extract

Notes to add my own voice to this recipe!

Directions

1. Preheat the oven to 400f degrees.

2. Combine all the ingredients in a large bowl.

3. Fill a greased muffin tin. or muffin cups. ¾ full of batter.

4. Bake for 15-20 minutes.

My Story

Food has always played an important role in my life. I believe that food connects people and gives us insight into different cultures and history. I have always been enamored by the intricacy of developing flavors and creating beautiful dishes. Throughout college, I found that cooking was what I turned to when the stress of school and work became too much. My roommates and I would experiment with different techniques and dishes ranging from chicken dishes to fresh French bread.

When I found myself battling anxiety, I turned to YouTube to learn more about food and cooking. I used these tutorials to channel that stressful energy and turn it into something beautiful and delicious. We all cope with stress in different ways - some don't eat at all, some eat too much. Thus, I strive to cook healthy alternatives that are delicious, to combat the unhealthy relationship that many of us have with food.

I found this recipe when my roommates and I were looking for a healthy alternative for muffins. They are best served toasted with a little bit of butter, and are great for breakfast!

BIO

Becca

Originally from San Diego. Becca is a recent graduate of Northeastern University. She is continuing her educational journey by pursuing her Master's Degree in Public Health from Northeastern University and eventually moving on to Physician Assistant (PA) school. She loves to help others and has held multiple roles doing so in the clinical setting. Becca loves Core Power Yoga, cooking, and being with her friends and family.

Alyssa's Snickerdoodles

Ingredients:

- 1½ cups sugar
- ½ cup unsalted butter, softened
- ½ cup shortening
- 2 eggs
- 2¾ cups all-purpose unbleached flour
- 2 tsp. cream of tartar
- 1 tsp. baking soda
- ¼ tsp. salt
- ¼ cup sugar
- 2 tsp. ground cinnamon

Notes to add my own voice to this recipe!

Directions

1. Preheat the oven to 400F degrees.

2. Combine 1 ½ cups of sugar. and the butter. shortening and eggs in a large bowl.

3. Stir in the flour. cream of tartar. baking soda and salt.

4. Shape the dough into 1¼-inch balls.

5. Mix ¼ cup of sugar and the cinnamon to create a cinnamon sugar mixture.

6. Roll the balls in the cinnamon sugar mixture. Place them two inches apart on an ungreased sheet.

7. Bake 8-10 minutes. or until set.

8. Remove the cookies from the sheet and cool on a wire rack.

My Story

I've never been one to be patient. If I could have any superpower, it would be to snap my fingers and have things accomplished. In elementary school, my friend brought my family some of these snickerdoodles for a family party. After the first sugary bite, I instantly fell in love! They were soft, sweet, and chewy...of course, I needed the recipe!

The following week, my mom brought me to the store and bought all the ingredients to make them. We measured all of the ingredients and mixed them together. We made sure to follow the recipe exactly, so that they turned out just right! But as we were making the cookies, all I can remember was checking the clock, constantly asking if they were done yet: "Why are they taking so long? We have to wait and chill them? Can't we just stick them in the oven and cook them?" I didn't understand that skipping the middle steps and going right to the end could ruin them. I knew what they tasted like, and I just wanted the perfectly baked cookies immediately! So of course, my mom had to explain that sometimes the best things in life are worth waiting for.

Life is not always as fast as we may want it to be, or how we expect it, but that's what makes it beautiful...because those are the kind of endings worth waiting for.

BIO

Alyssa Parker

Alyssa Parker, a newly married woman and dear longtime friend of the author, Dayna, has always loved to bake and cook. Alyssa graduated from Westfield State College in Westfield, MA, and has since built her life in Western MA, with her husband, Garett, and their 2-year-old English Chocolate Labrador dog, Hunter.

Andrea's Soft Baked Flour Chocolate Chip Cookies

Ingredients:

- 2 Tbsp. solid coconut oil
- 3 Tbsp. pure maple syrup
- 1 large egg
- 1 tsp. vanilla extract
- 2 cups almond flour
- ½ tsp. baking powder
- ¼ tsp. fine-grain sea salt
- ½ cup mini semi-sweet chocolate chips*

*or any other similar toppings that may be desired, such as craisins, dried cherries, or unsweetened coconut.

Notes to add my own voice to this recipe!

Directions

1. Preheat the oven to 375f degrees.

2. Line a baking sheet with parchment paper or a silicone mat. Set aside.

3. In a large bowl. combine the coconut oil and maple syrup. If the oil is every hard. microwave it for a few seconds until soft but not melted. Stir briskly with a whisk until the syrup and oil are mixed together - this may take one to two minutes.

4. Add the egg and vanilla. and whisk together until combined.

5. In a medium bowl. stir together the almond flour. baking powder. and salt. Add the flour mixture to the wet ingredients. and stir together with a wooden spoon until combined.

6. Stir in the chocolate chips and any other desired toppings.

7. Scoop the batter. one tablespoon at a time. onto the cookie sheet. Space two inches apart and press down gently with your fingers to flatten slightly.

8. Top each with a few additional chocolate chips. if desired.

9. Bake for 8-9 minutes. or until the edges are golden brown.

10. Remove the cookies from the oven and let cool for about 5 minutes. then transfer to a wire rack to cool completely.

My Story

Who doesn't love chocolate? I mean seriously love it...in our family we do. I also love to cook for people. Nothing says, "I really care for you, here's some love on a plate!" like something homemade does.

I have recently started to teach my 15-year-old daughter how to cook and bake. Working side by side, we are able to have really great mindful conversations about whatever comes to us. It is less intimidating standing next to each other.

She has seen me make birthday cakes for my staff and has asked me "Why are you making them a cake?" My answer is always, "Because it's their day to feel special and loved." She has seen me cooking meals when someone has had a bad day or has lost someone they care deeply about.

Being able to make someone smile or feel good about themselves is better than anything in the world. By doing so, you are saying "Hey, I got your back, I'm here for you."

My recipe is a very healthy one. We are very health-conscious in our house, and still love our sweets. And let's face it, sometimes you just need a cookie.

Enjoy, and thank you for this opportunity to share with you!

BIO

Andrea Foley

Andrea Foley is a hair stylist of 19 years, and hair styling just so happens to be one of her favorite things to do! She feels there is nothing better than making another person feel good about themselves, and she loves that she can do this every day. When she is not styling hair, you can find her spinning, running, reading, or spending time with her goofy family. Although her life may be busy and crazy, she loves every minute.

Marie Louise's Mohn Kipferl

Ingredients:

Dough
- 3½ cups bread flour
- ¼ cup sugar
- dash of salt
- 3 tsp. active dry yeast
- I cup milk. room temperature
- 1/3 cup unsalted butter. softened

Filling
- ½ cup milk
- ¼ cup sugar
- ¼ cup unsalted butter
- ½ cup ground poppy seeds
- I tsp. bourbon (for taste)
- Add small amounts of breadcrumbs at your own discretion. if filling looks too liquid

Notes to add my own voice to this recipe!

Directions

1. Preheat the oven to 350F degrees.

2. Combine the flour, sugar, and salt.

3. In a separate bowl, add the yeast to the milk, and whisk to mix well. Let it rest for 5 minutes.

4. Stir the flour mixture into the yeast and milk mixture, forming a dough.

5. Add the soft butter to the dough, then mix by hand, or at low to medium speed with a standing mixer, for about 10 minutes. The dough should be sticky, but nice to work with. Let it rest for approximately one hour.

6. Make the filling while the dough rests.

7. To make the filling, heat the milk with the sugar and butter. Stir in the poppy seeds while the mixture is still hot. Add the bourbon and whisk briefly. Let it cool.

8. When the dough is ready, roll it into rectangles, about one ounce at a time. Turn the rectangle so that one corner is facing you.

9. Put one full teaspoon of filling in the imaginary triangle between the top three corners. Fold the top corner over the filling, and roll up the dough gently. Take the last corner and press it against the roll.

10. Shape the Kipferl so that the corner is in the bottom middle of the Kip ferl (into a crescent moon shape). Place each Kipferl onto a baking sheet, and brush with a little milk.

11. Bake for about 20 minutes, until golden brown.

My Story

When Dayna first told me about her cookbook, I was intrigued. Not only because I love being inspired by new recipes, but also because I love to learn about the people behind them.

While it may be cliché, when I tell people I am from Austria, they tend to either think of "The Sound of Music" or the sweet treats that friends return with after they visit Vienna. In a similar fashion, I decided to contribute something "traditionally Austrian:" Kipferl. Although it is not a cake or strudel, it is one of my favorite things to make.

I found this recipe in an old family cookbook in my grandmother's kitchen. This recipe is like my grandmother: down-to-earth, doesn't want too much attention, and the dough rises best when the room is well-tempered.

When my grandmother passed away recently, I began to realize that I am more like her than I may have wanted to accept. Some characteristics that we shared may have seemed less obvious, but the love that we shared for baking was clearly overt. She not only loved baking, but also sharing. There's something about giving away some of what you created that makes it more special. Thus, I chose to contribute this recipe, as it is made to be shared (and easily tested - who doesn't want to try the treat they are going to bring to the party?).

Not only did I share my love of baking with my grandmother, but I also benefit from the art of baking in many other different ways. It has helped me to become more mindful, and has helped me to relieve stress. For example, in this recipe there are several moments of pause, where all you have to do is concentrate on measuring ingredients and following the directions at hand. Baking has also allowed me to express myself creatively. I love trying new recipes or combining traditional ideas with new flavors and hoping for a new product.

More than anything, though, baking has given me a sense of home. When there is a scent of a baked good in the air, I find that I become immediately more comfortable, even if I am 5,000 miles away from my family.

Baking has not only had these benefits for me, but I believe that its heart, the acts of creating and giving, is what makes baking so healing.

Taking care of one's health is a personal process. Similarly, there is no one recipe or formula that works for everyone. Although it can be a difficult journey of trial and error, coming up with a self-care routine that works for you can be both empowering and life changing.

The page below serves as an interactive exercise to help you understand and establish how to best prioritize your mental health.

Circle your answers below:

> I feel best in the morning / night.

> I find myself energized being with others / being alone.

> I make time for myself often / never.

> I do not know how to take care of my mental health. / I do know how to take care of my mental health, and I take care of it often.

> Creating goals for myself is easy / hard.

> I implement self-care routinely / rarely.

These questions - and your answers - are meant to help you reflect on how you can improve the time and space you take to care for your well-being.

Identifying when you feel your best can clue you in to an optimal time for when you can embrace a self-care routine. The second question should help you reflect on how to recharge.

Acknowledging if you know how to take time for yourself and whether or not you do is also a great step toward creating goals in self-care.

Regardless of the results of this quick quiz, everyone can benefit from establishing goals. Use the space below to list a short-term goal, a long-term goal, and the steps you will take to achieve each.

Short-term goal:

Steps:

Long-term goal:

Steps:

What happens if you achieve this goal? List immediate and future effects.

If you do not achieve this goal, how will you still care for yourself and celebrate that you worked toward a self-improvement goal?

Part 4

Loss, Change & Physical Ailment

Eve's Comfort Meringue Cookies

Ingredients:

- 4 egg whites, room temperature
- ½ tsp. cream of tartar
- 1 tsp. vanilla extract
- 1 cup sugar
- 1 cup chocolate chips (suggested: dark chocolate)

Notes to add my own voice to this recipe!

Directions

1. Preheat the oven to 350F degrees.

2. Put the four egg whites in a bowl and allow them to stand at room temperature for 30 minutes.

3. Line two cookie sheets with parchment paper.

4. Beat the egg whites until foamy, then add the cream of tartar and beat again.

5. Add the sugar, two tablespoons at a time, beating after each addition. Add the vanilla halfway through the process, and then continue to add the rest of the sugar two tablespoons at a time. At this point, the egg whites should be stiff.

6. Stir in the chocolate chips using a spoon or spatula.

7. Drop the dough by rounded teaspoons onto cookie sheets.

8. Put the cookies in the preheated oven, then turn the oven off.

9. Check on the cookies after eight hours - they should feel firm and not squishy. If they feel squishy, take them out of the oven and turn the oven on again to 350F for about 10 minutes. Put the cookies back in the oven and turn the oven off. They should be ready in an hour or two.

10. You can test the cookies' doneness by squeezing them, or by eating one, of course.

My Story

After my husband, Rocky, died, I was bereft. We had been married for 50 years, and for the last 25 we had worked for the same company and were together 24 hours a day, 7 days a week. The grief was overwhelming. I received advice from well-meaning friends and family on how to deal with it. Some of the advice was helpful and some wasn't, but none of it changed the fact that he was gone. What I wanted to do was get into bed and pull the covers over my head. What I did do was go into the kitchen. I always felt peaceful when I was baking something, so I looked for an easy recipe that didn't take much thought as long as it had chocolate chips in it. And so, I made comfort cookies - I named them that because they gave me comfort. Rocky never did much in the kitchen, but he thought I was the most talented baker in the world. I smiled when I thought of that. After I finished that batch, I made another batch, and then another. To this day, I am still making and eating those cookies.

The most important lesson I learned from this experience is that everyone is different. It sounds obvious, but to really accept this and not judge anyone for how they handle their life is a major thing to learn. If you have lost someone that you love, anything you feel is OK. Your feelings are your feelings - no right or wrong. Some people feel "better" in a year. Some people always have that hole in their heart where someone is missing. Some people try to concentrate on remembering the good things about that person. Some people like to remember everything that made up that missing life. Some widows remarry. Some go on the Internet to find love. Some are happy just being alone. So never apologize for what you feel about anything - you know best!

BIO

Eve Altman

Eve Altman is a 78-year-old mother of three, and grandmother of eight, one of whom is the author of this cookbook. She resides in Henderson, NV, and loves to read - sometimes three books at once. She also enjoys playing word games with family and friends on her iPad, as well as streaming the Acorn TV service. She loves to bake treats for the special people in her life.

Laurie's Extra-Ordinary Chocolate Cupcakes submitted by April Churchill

Ingredients:

Cupcakes
- 1 cup unbleached all-purpose flour
- ½ cup unsweetened cocoa powder
- ½ tsp. baking powder
- ¼ tsp. baking soda
- ½ tsp. salt
- ¾ cup granulated sugar
- 2 large eggs
- ½ cup milk
- ¼ cup canola oil
- 1 tsp. vanilla extract
- ½ cup mini chocolate chips
- ½ cup mini white chocolate chips

Buttercream Frosting
- 6 Tbsp. butter
- 3½ cups powdered sugar
- 4 Tbsp. whole milk
- 1 tsp. vanilla extract
- 1 pinch salt

Notes to add my own voice to this recipe!

Directions

<u>Cupcakes</u>

1. Preheat the oven to 350F degrees.

2. Combine the flour, cocoa, baking powder, baking soda, and salt in a bowl, and stir.

3. In another bowl, whisk together the sugar, eggs, milk, oil, and vanilla.

4. Add the dry ingredients to the wet ingredients, then add in the mini chocolate chips.

5. Fill the muffin cups halfway, and bake about 20 minutes.

<u>Frosting</u>

1. Mix the butter, powdered sugar, milk, vanilla, and salt in a bowl. Using an electric mixer, beat the ingredients together until fluffy, adding additional milk or powdered sugar as necessary.

2. Spread or pipe the frosting on the cooled cupcakes.

My Story

Whenever I would arrive for a family dinner at my oldest sister, Laurie's, house, I could smell the delicious foods she had cooked and baked for the occasion. Being the youngest of five children, I was spoiled by my family's love, and especially by Laurie's. Laurie always made my favorite foods: mashed potatoes with gravy and her famous chocolate cupcakes with buttercream frosting. After any dinner at her house, my sisters and I would be thrilled when Laurie would proudly present her cupcakes on the table for us to enjoy. Laurie knew how much we loved her cupcakes and made sure she had extras for her little sisters. I don't think any of us realized that these cupcakes were made from simple ingredients, but we knew they were created with love. They always tasted and looked delicious, and I can remember her smiling when we would enjoy them.

Laurie lived her life by the words of her favorite country singer, Tim McGraw: she "lived like [she] was dying." She was diagnosed with cystic fibrosis when she was 13 years old, and had lived an incredible life since then, loving with her whole heart. Even though she rarely mentioned being sick or dying, she lived her life like that song: knowing what was most important. Our daily phone calls always ended with "Goodbye, I love you." She made sure we knew how much she loved us. One cold March morning, Laurie passed away. Although we knew the inevitable end of her illness, we still could not imagine living a day without hearing her voice or being in her loving presence. My family and I stumbled through the next weeks, grieving, hugging, talking, and coping together. We talked about Laurie often, remembering how she made us laugh, how she encouraged us to make the right choices, offered advice when we made mistakes, and how she could transform the ordinary parts of life into the extraordinary, just with her love. One of the most important ways we decided we would keep her memory alive was to celebrate her birthday as a family and recreate the cupcakes she always made us.

Every year on Laurie's birthday, I head to the grocery store and buy the ingredients to make her extraordinary cupcakes. Once they are baked, we sing happy birthday as a family and honor her memory by sharing stories about her. We tell our children how much she loved us, how she liked to dance like nobody was watching, and how she lived her life to the fullest.

Although these cupcakes will never taste as delicious as hers, continuing her baking legacy is our way to honor her memory forever.

BIO

April Churchill

April Churchill is the founder of the non-profit organization. "The Reflower Project." "The Reflower Project" repurposes event flowers and delivers them to community centers in the Boston area. Born and raised on Boston's South Shore. April grew into a woman who loves being of service to others. She has a wonderful husband. Tom. and four daughters all named after flowers. She also has many pets. As a Registered Nurse. April has come to learn the importance of physical, spiritual, and emotional wellness. April enjoys roses. conversation. and family. and knows the importance of a simple act of kindness.

Notes, Thoughts & Goals

Michael's Mini-Cupcake Pies

Ingredients:

Mini-Cupcake Pies

- 2 boxes vanilla cake mix
- 4 eggs (or amount listed on cake mix box)
- 2/3 cup oil (or amount listed on cake mix box)

Frosting

- ½ cup unsalted butter. softened
- 3 Tbsp. milk
- 1 tsp. vanilla
- 2-3 cups powdered sugar
- 1 Tbsp. food coloring (purple pictured here. but can use any color)
- sprinkles (pink sprinkles pictured here. but can use any color)

Notes to add my own voice to this recipe!

Directions

Cupcake pies

1. Preheat the oven to 350f degrees.

2. Follow the directions on the boxes of vanilla cake mix to make the batter. incorporating the eggs and oil per the cake mix directions.

3. Mix and roll the batter into small balls and gently flatten.

4. Bake for 8-10 minutes.

Frosting

1. Mix the frosting ingredients together. adding more milk or powdered sugar. if necessary. to reach the desired consistency.

2. Add the food coloring and mix in.

3. Frost the small cake balls once they are baked and cooled.

4. Put the cake balls together to make "small pies."

5. Add the sprinkles for design.

My Story

My name is Michael Fine, and I practice the magical 26 & 2 yoga series almost daily, and have done so for practically six years. This beautiful series figuratively and literally saved my life!I was rescued by this healing, therapeutic yoga after living my life in chronic, debilitating, 365-24/7 residual limb pain, the result of a head-on collision, at approximately 40 miles per hour, with a large, red concrete truck in April of 2010.

I was on my way to work that fateful day when that truck crossed the center line, traveled up the hood of my car, continued through my windshield, and traumatically amputated my left arm cleanly at the shoulder. After surviving such a horrific accident and living in chronic pain, in conjunction with the loss of both of my beloved parents within that same short timeframe, I developed severe depression and an addiction to painkillers. All of this culminated in a suicide attempt. I was left completely empty and in search of a new way to live and move forward. As you have likely guessed, that way forward was, is, and will likely always be, my yoga practice. This beautiful, healing 26 & 2 series.

Since the day I lost my left arm, I have completely felt as if it were still attached to my body. However, my phantom arm feels like it is encased in a block of ice and being continuously squeezed in a vise. This is my reality. This is my life. I generally live at between five and seven on the proverbial '1-10 pain scale.' My existence really centers around doing all I can to live at as low a number on that scale as possible. The 'external triggers,' or factors that exacerbate the pain, are outside of my control (e.g. weather, pressure, and temperature fluctuations). Fortunately, however, the 'internal triggers,' (e.g. feeling stress, tension, and anxiety) are completely within my control to manipulate. In an effort to learn to do so, I tried many different healing modalities like Reiki, Cranial Sacral Therapy, LifeLine and other energy work, acupuncture, sensory deprivation flotation, massage therapy, etc. All those techniques are important and effective tools in my arsenal to battle life in chronic pain. However, the single most effective weapon that I possess, as you have likely guessed, is my daily yoga practice! In my six years of practice, in my likely 2,000+ classes, there has never been even one class in which I haven't felt less pain after those glorious 90 minutes than before that class started! To date, I haven't found anything else that helps me in this way. As such, I call this yoga practice and series a universal truth. In other words, this yoga is a constant, like gravity! This yoga practice is science! The mental and spiritual clarity that this magical 90-minute moving meditation provides is further icing on the yogic cake!

The most beautiful thing about this series is that almost anyone can do it! In the words of a living legend and one of my many mentors, the incomparable Mary Jarvis, "All you need to do this yoga is a spine!" Two arms are completely optional! I plan to continue this practice for the rest of my life! In that regard, I recently took the next step in the advancement of my practice by attending teacher training in September 2017. I am proud to be a newly-minted and certified "500 Hour Hatha Yoga - Core 26 Instructor" by Craig Villani's exceptional Raja Yoga Academy in Huntington Beach, CA.

My primary goal moving forward is to inspire and change the minds of all those who believe that they can't practice this yoga for reasons many of you have likely heard time and time again: "I am too old, too fat, too inflexible, too sick, allergic to heat, etc." My yoga journey is truly beginning as I start to teach and share my love of this yoga with others, with the sole objective and ultimate goal of inspiring and empowering people to do what the human body, mind, and spirit were truly designed to do: that is to heal!

BIO

Michael Fine

Michael Fine is a recovering attorney, and now a happy, grateful Hatha Yoga Instructor. He believes we each possess the innate ability to heal physically, mentally, and spiritually. He believes that with proper wholesome nutrition, hydration, lifestyle, and yoga, our bodies return to homeostasis, the natural byproduct of which is that we heal, inside out, bones to skin, fingertips to toes!

Reem's Rainbow Sprinkle Chocolate Chip Cookies

Ingredients:

- 1 cup unsalted butter, melted and cooled for at least 10 minutes
- 1¼ cups brown sugar, tightly packed
- ½ cup white sugar
- 1 large egg + 1 yolk, room temperature
- 1½ tsp. vanilla extract
- 2¾ cups all-purpose flour
- 2 tsp. cornstarch
- 1 tsp. baking soda
- ¾ tsp. salt
- 1¾ cups chocolate chips
- 1 cup rainbow sprinkles

Notes to add my own voice to this recipe!

Directions

1. Preheat the oven to 350F degrees.

2. Combine the melted butter and sugars in a large bowl. Stir very well.

3. Add the egg and egg yolk. and stir well.

4. Stir in the vanilla extract. Set aside.

5. In a medium bowl. whisk together the flour. cornstarch. baking soda. and salt.

6. Gradually add the flour mixture to the wet ingredients. and stir well. so that all the flour is absorbed.

7. Stir in the chocolate chips and sprinkles.

8. Place the dough in the refrigerator. and chill for 30 minutes.

9. Line the cookie sheets with parchment paper.

10. Scoop the dough by rounded 1½ tablespoons onto the prepared cookie sheets. placing them at least 2 inches apart.

11. Bake for 11 minutes.

12. Allow the cookies to cool completely on the cookie sheets.

My Story

Life changed dramatically for me when I moved to the United States. I moved to the U.S. with my family when I was 13 years old. I was born in Iraq, but I lived in Syria for three years because it was safer than living in Iraq at the time. I was so nervous to move because it meant I needed to become accustomed to new food, clothes, people and most challenging of all, a new language that was very different from Arabic. I recall having the same reoccurring thought in my head at night before moving to the U.S.: how could I go to school if I was not fluent in English?

My experience of moving to a new country is a little bit of a blur, which may be due to the culture shock I experienced. I still remember how I felt at the beginning: worried and anxious about starting school. I felt like I wasted so many years of my life going to school in Iraq, because when I moved, I felt as though I instantly forgot everything I had learned in Iraq and Syria. This made me very nervous and concerned because it meant that I had so much to learn. Before moving, I attended school in Syria as a ninth-grader, but when I moved, I had to take a test to determine what grade I would be placed in within a traditional U.S. school. During the test, I recall being asked questions and knowing the answers, but not remembering the English words to write down. I was given a few seconds to respond on a piece of paper. I can remember my face feeling hot and tears welling up in my eyes, because I thought that doing poorly on this test would mean that I would be put in a lower grade than was appropriate for me. Ultimately, though, I was put into eighth grade.

School in the U.S. was different, to say the least. In Iraq, students were grouped according to age rather than levels of intelligence. Public schools had uniforms and were strict. Classes were hard and teachers did not care if students understood the material, so long as they could memorize it. I struggled to understand the material in each subject, and felt nervous when taking tests. I went to an all-female school because public schools were segregated in Iraq. I was shy and did not like to communicate with or meet new people. I mostly stayed with my twin sister for safety.

When I came to the United States, I was shocked at how much teachers cared about their students. I found school much easier and more enjoyable. For the first time in my life, I stopped feeling nervous when I took a test, because I understood the material. In the eighth grade, I took a class called ESL A, for people who knew very little English (ESL stands for English as a Second Language). I worked myself up to ESL B and ESL C during freshman and sophomore years of high school. I even skipped ESL D, which was the last level for ESL students. My teacher recommended me to take Honors English, and I have taken those classes since then.

Education has been such a huge part of my life due to my background. However, having graduated from college and now taking time off while joining the AmeriCorps, I am learning that there are other important things in life as well. Every now and then, moving to the U.S. seems unreal, like a dream. Sometimes I can't help but wonder what my life would be like if I had stayed in Iraq or Syria, but ultimately, I feel thankful to be living here.

BIO

Reem Ahmad

Reem Ahmad was born in Baghdad, Iraq, in 1995, and moved to the United States with her family in 2008. She graduated from Salem State University with a Bachelor's Degree in biology. One area of biology Reem is especially interested in is the field of genetics. She has also taken interest in nutrition and baking. Some of her hobbies include listening to music and playing "Just Dance."

Notes, Thoughts & Goals

Lorin's Chocolate Bark

Ingredients:

- 35-40 saltine crackers
- 1 cup unsalted butter
- 1 cup light brown sugar
- 8 oz. semisweet chocolate chips

Notes to add my own voice to this recipe!

Directions

1. Preheat the oven to 425F degrees.

2. Line a large jelly roll pan with aluminum foil, and spray with nonstick spray. Arrange the saltines in a single layer, salt side down.

3. In a medium saucepan, melt the butter and brown sugar together, and boil until it becomes a caramel color (this will take a few minutes).

4. Remove the mixture from the heat and pour it over the crackers in the jelly roll pan, covering them evenly.

5. Put the jelly roll pan into oven, and bake for 3-5 minutes, until bubbly.

6. Remove the pan from the oven and pour the chocolate chips over the crackers.

7. When the chips melt, spread them over the crackers with a knife.

8. Transfer the pan to the freezer for 15-20 minutes, or until cold.

9. Break the chocolate bark into small pieces.

My Story

I am a mother, I am a cancer survivor, I am a wife, a daughter, a sister, a cousin, an aunt, and a friend. What I am not, is someone who is comfortable in the kitchen. The memories I have of my mother's baking envelop me in warmth and love. So it makes sense that I gravitated towards my life partner, Vicki, who is amazing in the kitchen. She has a wide range of talent, from homemade chicken soup and lasagna, to BBQ anything, and she is also an incredible baker. I am in awe of her confidence, especially when cooking for our picky children. A week doesn't go by that she is not making some yummy treat to put in our children's lunches. The smell, the love, and the inspiration that come from her kitchen are all things I cherish each day.

It took a long time to find Vicki. It took even longer to have our children. When our family was complete and our adventure was beginning, I got breast cancer. I didn't eat for months, mouth sores everywhere, a metallic taste in my mouth, the pain, the hopelessness of every meal that I sat at that table. Vicki tried anything and everything, even marijuana brownies, to no avail. As the sores started to heal, as the taste came back to normal, my head lifted and I was finally ready to eat what my love was going to make me. It all tasted so good again. After nine months of treatment, I was on the mend and our family was now ready to continue our adventure. I don't have one specific recipe to contribute - I love everything Vicki makes. She never backs down from a challenge, and she is the reason we all love food so much.

BIO

Lorin Altman

Lorin Altman is the proud aunt of the author of this cookbook. She is 54 years old and married to her wonderful partner. Vicki. She also has two beautiful children. Jacob and Jenna. and a dog. Rosie. For over 20 years. Lorin has been a Valet Attendant at a local Hotel Casino in her hometown of Las Vegas. NV. She is also currently the PTA President at her daughter's school. and a part-time tutor. Her interests include anything that has to do with her children. golf. travel. and spending time with family and friends.

Janaial's Apple Crisp

Ingredients:

- 10 cups apples. peeled. cored. and sliced
- 1 cup white sugar
- 1 cup + 1 Tbsp. all-purpose flour
- 1 tsp. ground cinnamon
- ½ cup water
- 1 cup quick-cooking oats
- 1 cup packed brown sugar
- ¼ tsp. baking powder
- ¼ tsp. baking soda
- ½ cup unsalted butter. melted

Notes to add my own voice to this recipe!

Directions

1. Preheat the oven to 350F degrees.

2. Place the sliced apples in a 9x13-inch pan.

3. Mix the white sugar, 1 tablespoon of flour, and the ground cinnamon together in a bowl, and sprinkle the mixture over the apples.

4. Pour the water evenly over the apples and flour mixture.

5. Combine the oats, 1 cup of flour, brown sugar, baking powder, baking soda, and melted butter together. Crumble it evenly over the apple mixture.

6. Bake for 45 minutes.

My Story

If you asked me 15 years ago whether I would suffer from depression because I could not provide for my three-year-old son, I would have said, "No, that will never be me."

When I decided to start my family, I thought I had done everything right. I grew up in a neighborhood that was full of violence, drugs, and alcohol: a place where it was easy to fall into the cracks of failure. However, I knew I wanted more for myself, so I stayed involved in positive community activities, finished high school, gained experience in a field I was passionate about, went to college, and graduated. Never in a million years would I have thought that just a few years later I would be homeless and job searching with little to no income.

Looking back on it all, I sometimes feel guilty: I know a lot of women who were, and still are, in this same situation but have even more children to provide for. However, I never gave up, I reached my goals to acquire self-sufficiency, and I survived.

My name is Janaial, and I am not just an employee of "Dress to Success," I am the Director of Operations within the Boston chapter. "Dress for Success" is an international non-profit organization that helps homeless women find jobs and build careers and confidence. The organization not only provides women with clothing to interview for jobs, but also with mentoring, interview skills, and classes.

Most mornings, I wake up and think of what I am thankful for. First, for my beautiful son, who is my personal comedian and makes me laugh every day, even when I'm sad. Second, for my family, who supports me in everything I do and loves me unconditionally. Finally, I am thankful for the strong and courageous women who walk through the door at "Dress for Success: Boston." They always remind me: I am so much like them. A woman who was once struggling to keep a roof over her family's head, to put food on the table, with no employment. Yes, it's been a long road for me, with many challenges and accomplishments, but I know the work that I do to help women persevering through their lives is more than just my job – it is my truth.

BIO

Janaial Robinson

Janaial Robinson is the Director of Operations at Dress for Success Boston. a nonprofit agency that provides interview clothing and self-confidence to women. Previously. she served as a peer leader to teens at the YMCA. and at Morgan Memorial Goodwill Industries as a Master Mentor for ten years. In this role. she developed an education-based curriculum for 46 girls ages nine to seventeen. and taught them social skills to succeed. A creative self-starter with strong communication skills and leadership abilities. Janaial enjoys helping others and making a difference. In her free time. she enjoys being around her big family. immediate and extended. who are scarily close. She also enjoys being silly with her son. who's her personal comedian. and getting lost in the world of a good book.

Notes, Thoughts & Goals

Jordan's Eclair Pie

Ingredients:

- 3 cups milk
- 2 boxes instant French Vanilla Pudding mix
- 1 (8oz.) container whipped topping (such as Cool Whip)
- 1 box graham crackers
- ¼ cup evaporated milk
- 1/3 cup powdered baking chocolate
- ¾ cup sugar
- 8 Tbsp. unsalted butter or margarine
- 1 tsp. vanilla

Notes to add my own voice to this recipe!

Directions

1. Mix the milk and pudding on low speed until thick.

2. Add the whipped topping. and mix well.

3. In a 9x13-inch pan. layer whole graham crackers. half of the pudding mixture. more graham crackers. then the remaining pudding mixture. then another layer of graham crackers.

4. On low heat. in a saucepan. heat the evaporated milk. chocolate. and sugar until dissolved. stirring frequently. Then add the butter. stirring until melted and bubbly.

5. Remove from the heat and add the vanilla.

6. Spread the mixture evenly over the top of the pie. and refrigerate it overnight.

My Story

I am 15 years old now, but when I was in seventh grade, I met this guy. We started dating and at first everything was fine. In fact, I was so happy to be a part of his life. However, after a couple of months he changed a lot and started putting pressure on me to do things I didn't want to do. He didn't listen or respect me anymore - it felt abusive. I think this is where my depression and anxiety came from. My feelings got worse every day, and soon I felt I wanted to harm myself or take my life. But at the end of 7th grade, I got the opportunity to move somewhere new.

I never told anyone why I was moving, but I have come to terms with the fact that it was due to the bullying and the guy. When I told my friends that I was moving, I lost them all. I felt they hated me for it. Although it was hard, I am so happy to say that I am doing much better! Yes, I still struggle, but I have not hurt myself since the move. I am now in an amazing relationship with someone who wants the best for me, and I feel genuinely happy. I know I will always miss the friends that I lost in seventh grade, but I see now that the loss is theirs, and I am happy to be in this new place.

Notes, Thoughts & Goals

Sarah's Lemon Bars

Ingredients:

Pie Crust
- 1 cup unsalted butter, softened
- 2 cups all-purpose flour
- ½ cup white sugar

Lemon Curd
- 1½ cups white sugar
- ½ cup all-purpose flour
- 4 eggs
- 2 lemons, juiced
- ½ cup powdered sugar

Notes to add my own voice to this recipe!

Directions

Pie Crust

1. Preheat the oven to 350F degrees.

2. In a medium bowl, blend together the butter, flour, and sugar.

3. Press into the bottom of an ungreased 9x13-inch pan.

4. Bake for 15-20 minutes, or until firm and golden.

Lemon Curd

1. In another bowl, whisk together the sugar and flour.

2. Whisk in the eggs and lemon juice.

3. Pour the mixture over the baked crust, and bake for an additional 20 minutes.

4. Shake the powdered sugar on top for decoration.

My Story

"Who is calling me from a random number on a Saturday afternoon?" I thought to myself, annoyed, as I answered the phone. I was just lying down for an afternoon nap when I got the phone call that would change my life forever. The woman on the other end of the phone explained she was calling from UCLA Medical Center. I interrupted her, stating I knew I had an appointment coming up and that I would be there. She then said, "No, this is about a transplant. We have a match for you." My heart stopped and I jumped out of bed. Thousands of thoughts rushed through my head... I was getting new lungs; I would finally be able to breathe again.

I walked into UCLA Ronald Reagan Medical Center the next morning, full of emotions: nervous, anxious, excited, relieved, and afraid. My surgery was scheduled for 10am, if the lungs were in good shape and looked healthy. As I waited to hear whether or not it was a "go," I prepared myself for the worst, just in case. The doctor came in, stating that the donor family needed more time with the donor, who was on a ventilator. I thought to myself, "Oh no, they're going to back out. I'm not going to get these lungs." About 20 minutes later, they told me it was a "go" and immediately wheeled me into the Operating Room. I didn't even have time to think about what was happening. I was placed on a cold, silver table in a 50-degree room with masked people, noisy machines, and equipment everywhere. I was hooked up to a million devices, and slowly slipped into anesthesia. Two days later, I woke up in the Intensive Care Unit (ICU). The hardest part was over, so I thought.

I now had new lungs after living with Cystic Fibrosis for so long, but major surgery doesn't come without challenges. I had a massive mucus plug that blocked my airways after surgery, and I started suffocating. Doctors and nurses rushed in and reintubated me. They did a bronchoscopy, which cleared my lungs and throat of secretions, and then I woke up again, swollen. The doctors found that my veins and vessels were very constricted from previous IVs so they then put me back under anesthesia to go in and open up my vessels. I was finally on the mend, when they noticed a hematoma. They sedated me again and took out the blood clot. They then found fluid in my lungs and proceeded to drain it. After each procedure, I hoped that it would be the last one, but they didn't seem to end. I felt defeated, exhausted, and hopeless.

When in a hospital, you tend to lose all autonomy and control. You are on everyone else's schedule. You go in for tests when they're ready for you, they take vitals and labs at all hours of the morning, they poke and prod you when you're trying to sleep, and doctors and nurses talk about you right in front of you. There were many times I felt invisible, just a body, with no say in my care. I was so grateful for this beautiful gift, but I started to wonder if this was all worth it.

Transplant is a whole lifestyle change and a lifelong commitment. I'm now immunosuppressed for the rest of my life, putting me at high risk of infection. I now take 40 pills a day for the rest of my life. I now have diabetes from the steroids, so I had to learn how to count carbohydrates and take insulin. I can no longer eat sushi, raw foods, deli meats, or at salad bars or buffets. I'm not allowed to have flowers in my house, or any animals with scales, and I'm not allowed to go in pools, hot tubs, or water parks. There are so many rules after transplant that I felt overwhelmed, anxious, and exhausted. But humans are very adaptable creatures, and now here I am, months later, loving my new lungs and my new life. There are still hurdles to overcome: medication adjustments, side effects from the medications, clinic visits, weekly blood draws, and other procedures. However, looking at the overall picture, I am extremely lucky and grateful just to take a deep breath again. To run again, to walk up the stairs again, and to live my new life to the fullest.

BIO

Sarah Albright

Sarah Albright is a 26-year-old New York native currently living in sunny Los Angeles. CA. Sarah works as a pulmonary rehabilitation coordinator at a local hospital. but will be starting a PhD program in health psychology this upcoming fall. For fun. she loves to travel. bake delicious goodies. read. be creative. and spend time with her friends. Sarah also has a small business making mosaics from broken jewelry. beads. and shells.

Notes, Thoughts & Goals

Nick's Caramel Peanut Butter Fudge

Ingredients:

Bottom Layer
- 1 cup milk chocolate chips
- ¼ cup butterscotch chips
- ¼ cup creamy peanut butter

Filling
- ¼ cup unsalted butter
- 1 cup white sugar
- ¼ cup evaporated milk
- 1½ cups marshmallow crème
- ¼ cup creamy peanut butter
- 1 tsp. vanilla extract
- 1½ cups salted peanuts. chopped

Caramel
- 1 (14 oz.) package individually wrapped caramels. unwrapped
- ¼ cup heavy cream

Top Layer
- 1 cup milk chocolate chips
- ¼ cup butterscotch chips
- ¼ cup creamy peanut butter

Notes to add my own voice to this recipe!

Directions

Bottom Layer
1. Lightly grease a 9x13-inch dish.

2. Combine the milk chocolate chips, butterscotch chips, and peanut butter in a small saucepan over low heat. Cook and stir until melted and smooth. Spread evenly in the prepared dish. Refrigerate until set.

Filling
1. In a heavy saucepan over medium-high heat, melt the butter. Stir in the sugar and evaporated milk. Bring to a boil, and let boil for five minutes.

2. Remove the saucepan from the heat, and stir in the marshmallow crème, peanut butter, and vanilla.

3. Fold in the peanuts. Spread this mixture over the bottom layer, and return to the refrigerator until set.

Caramel
1. Combine the caramels and cream in a medium saucepan over low heat.

2. Cook and stir until melted and smooth. Spread over the filling. Chill until set.

Top Layer
1. In a small saucepan over low heat, combine the milk chocolate chips, butterscotch chips, and peanut butter. Cook and stir until melted and smooth. Spread over the caramel layer.

2. Chill for one hour before cutting into 1-inch squares.

My Story

Hi, I'm Nick Zone. I'm one of the most positive people I know: it's what I strive for. In some ways, I'm not growing up. Unfortunately, that isn't sustainable. In 2017, a misadventure shook me to my foundation, and now I feel its struggles every day. Struggles to get back to my old happy self. To face these seemingly normal life challenges.

The big event that shook up my life happened in January 2017. It was quite a way to start the year. I was driving to work in the first hours of an icy snowstorm. A pair of bigger, heavier cars lost control and banged me up pretty severely. From what I've been told, a state trooper and some off-duty EMTs were able to pry open my car and keep me from dying. I'd like to think I was fighting, too. I don't give up easily. Over the course of the next month, I can only really remember feelings, imagery, and the exceptional moments. See, that's the tricky part about head injuries. Everything gets foggy or forgotten. I forgot the strangest things, like hunger and sleepiness...kind of hit reset on my whole character. All of a sudden I had new emotions and no coping techniques. What was this disgusting neediness and jealousy? Sometimes I just cried or overreacted, and then I noticed something cool happening: I was learning and adapting. If I fell asleep so quickly that I fell out of my own chair, then the next day I yawned and went to bed. If I went a whole day without eating, then the next day my stomach rumbled for chicken parm. If one day made me cry, then the next day I was ok with that, accepted it, and moved on to whatever was next. Our evolution has solutions built in, and as we grow up, we face all sorts of things that we learn from. We can beat anything and all of it. It's what makes us the top and most dangerous species: problem solving, endurance, and ferocity, but also care and laughter.

While I was recovering, and I still sort of am, I faced so much at once. Everyone is so patient with me, but I am driven. Yeah, a lot of the time it's too much, and I break. Then the next day is new and I put it back together. You begin to realize that you can get pretty good at it. Learning that you are better and stronger now than before. I look at it as fun: it's like a puzzle or game. I get to rewatch all my old favorite shows, re-taste my favorite foods, and rework my admittedly inferior writing. I get to make myself better. And bonus! I get the rewards: my improved, happier life. Maybe even some fun stuff, some well-deserved satisfaction and love. We will see, because I intend to make it.

BIO

Nick Zone

Nick Zone, lover of fall (solely for cider donuts), works as an educator at Nature's Classroom, where he teaches kids about science and nature. He absolutely loves his job and seeing the look on the faces of the kids he meets as they hold a salamander or when a CFL bulb lights up next to a plasma ball. He also loves playing Halo on Xbox with his buddies across the country.

Notes, Thoughts & Goals

Ruth's Almond Cookies

Ingredients:

- ½ cup unsalted butter, softened
- ½ cup white sugar
- 1 egg
- ½ cup ground almonds
- 2 tsp. amaretto liquor
- 1¼ cups all-purpose flour
- ¼ cup peanut butter
- ¼ cup coconut flakes

Notes to add my own voice to this recipe!

Directions

1. Preheat the oven to 400f degrees.

2. In a large bowl. cream together the butter and sugar.

3. Beat in the egg. amaretto. and almonds.

4. Gradually mix in the flour until well blended.

5. Drop the batter by teaspoonsful. 2 inches apart. on ungreased cookie sheets.

6. Bake 5-8 minutes. or until the cookies are lightly colored.

7. Cool. then add a thin layer of peanut butter.

8. Sprinkle with coconut flakes.

My Story

Motherhood. Being a mother is something I've always dreamed of and worked for - the end goal of my existence. So when I found out I was pregnant at 21, I was happy. My happiness soon diminished when reality began to set in. I was 21, still a full-time college student working a part-time job and getting financial support from my parents. Oh, my parents. They would be devastated when they learned their only child, who was pursuing a career and going to college, would soon have a child of her own. The boyfriend was no help either. He, too, had just turned 21 and was living at a college in New Hampshire. And on top of that, we had only been a month into dating when this all occurred. It was a shock to us both, but more of a burden to him. I found myself second-guessing my decision, when initially I had already told myself I'd keep it.

During that time, I remember feeling emotionless. I had become a zombie, day in and day out. I was just doing what I thought those around me felt would be best for me, for the situation. But how could they know what was best for me? I remember after the abortion feeling a void deep in my heart and soul. Because there I was again, alone. When I had been pregnant, at least I never felt alone - I knew there was something else that was always with me and loved me as much as I loved it. For months, I didn't feel like myself. I had isolated myself to try to make sense of what had just occurred and what I had done. I second-guessed that decision every single day. It was the most emotionally draining experience I had ever gone through, and I felt so alone.

After months of these feelings, I reached out for help. I started seeing a counselor that was provided through my school, and it's incredible how talking to a complete stranger about my most intimate experience made all the diffrence.

I heard myself talk, and oftentimes this was where I would find my solutions. My healing process had begun, and it continues to this day. I don't think I've ever been the same since that experience. I've become better. I've become more compassionate, more loving, more grateful, because you never know the silent battles someone is facing. If there's one thing I've learned through this experience, it is to own your story. It is what builds you, it is what molds you, it is nothing to be ashamed of. In the beginning, I was ashamed of sharing my story, but now I own it and I share it, because not only does it help me heal, but I know another woman out there has gone through the same thing and needs to find her own strength to overcome it. I hope that by sharing my story, I can give those women a bit of strength and faith to find themselves again and start their own healing process.

Sarah's Oreo Fudge Brownies

Ingredients:

- 4 large eggs
- 1 ¼ cups of cocoa
- 1 tsp salt
- 1 tsp baking powder
- 1 Tbsp vanilla extract
- 1 cup (2 sticks) unsalted butter
- 2 ¼ cups sugar
- 1 ½ cups Flour
- 1 container of hot fudge (for ice cream)
- 2 cups of Oreo Sandwich Cookies

Notes to add my own voice to this recipe!

Directions

1. Preheat the oven to 350F.

2. Crack 4 eggs into a bowl and beat them at a medium speed with cocoa. salt. baking powder and vanilla for about 1 minute or until smooth. You can do this while melting the butter separately for the next step.

3. In a medium-sized bowl. melt the butter then add the sugar and stir to combine. Heat the mixture until the sugar dissolves.

4. Add the flour and Oreos until smooth.

5. Spoon the batter into a greased pan (9 x 13 suggested). Drizzle the container of hot fudge over the batter.

6. Bake the brownies for 30 minutes.

7. Let cool and enjoy.

Volvulus

A memorable feeling was how exhausting it was to walk at first. My "walking team" would accompany me, one person pushing the IV and another by my side. That first day I could only do a little lap and would go back to the hospital room, lay down, and instantly pass out. I remember thinking I can't believe I ran 9 miles last Saturday, and now I'm struggling to walk down this hall. Then, and even now, it's hard to grasp how randomly this event occurred. How I went to work, went for a run, then BOOM I couldn't even stand up to go to the bathroom by myself.

I remember when they removed my dressing and I saw my incision for the first time. Twenty-three staples up my midline in a Harry Potter-esque lightning bolt. It was so freaky to see on my own body, a symbol of what transpired the last six days. I will forever be grateful to the surgical team, who discovered this anomaly in my otherwise healthy 26 year old body. After 3.5 days in the hospital, an unnecessary appendectomy, and numerous other tests and exams, they finally diagnosed, and ultimately removed, a Cecal Volvulus. A cecal volvulus is a rare obstruction of the small intestine due to a twist on itself. According to my doctors, it occurs in only 1-1.5% of all adult intestinal obstructions. Long story short, I was very lucky to be alive.

Being a Physical Therapist of 2 years, I knew that returning to my active self would be slower than I'd like. What I wasn't prepared for, however, was the mental battle. After surgery, my body improved daily. Eventually, the NG tube and Foley catheter were removed, and before I knew it, I was discharged home, however I had several restrictions. My diet was to include soft, bland, foods only, and I could lift no greater than ten pounds. This prevented me from returning to work in any capacity, as I would be unable to move patients or demonstrate exercises properly. I was instructed to rest. While this may sound nice to some, to me it was the hardest part of my recovery. The disability leave tested me.

I was, and still am, an on-the-go person. I was spending my free time training for my first half marathon, going on adventure trips to Utah, or mountain biking around the reservoir. Living in the foothills of the Colorado Rocky Mountains; the activity and adventure were like air. During recovery, I felt like a huge piece of my identity was stripped from me. I was left with only my mind and soft, bland foods. As the weeks proceeded, my thoughts started to spiral. I found myself feeling worthless, burdensome, and alone. I grew angry; at others, at the debilitating tightness in my back forcing me to lay down, at my situation. I would wake up crying, and turned the anger on myself. I was frustrated that I wasn't mentally stronger. I became discouraged by my impatience. Knowing the physical healing was temporary, I would minimize my plight, comparing and telling myself it's not even that bad. When people asked how I was doing, I would tell them I was doing well; because I wanted to be, and because I wanted them to see me as a strong fighter who was recovering splendidly.

Ultimately, I did recover splendidly. Yes, because my body healed, and I did eventually run a half marathon, but I only got to that point because I decided to address my mentality. What truly helped me recover from this crazy, 1-1.5% chance thing was other people; and the turning point mentally was when I let them in. My parents and boyfriend spent a week with me and never let me stay down too long. My sister called every day and refused to take "I'm doing fine" for an answer. My best friend physically removed me from our apartment, drove me to the reservoir, and sat me down with a book while she worked. When you're left with nothing but your thoughts, your mind can take you places you never knew were there. Just like getting lost on a trail, I was having difficulty finding my way out of an unfamiliar place alone. For me, I leaned on those who loved me, because I needed them. I realized that what I was going through was worthy of their attention. Without the people who helped me through a tough time, I would still be wandering in the dark. It's ok to let someone else help you out of the darkness, or at least turn a light on, for a little while, until you can find the trail again.

BIO

Sarah Johnson

Sarah is a 29 year old New York native currently living in Cambridge, MA after spending two years living and working as a Physical Therapist in Fort Collins, Colorado. Sarah now works in greater Boston where she is the Clinical Director of an outpatient physical therapy office. Sarah's interests lie in Sport's Medicine Rehabilitation, where she finds great fulfillment in helping others get back to what they love. When she is not out traveling with her adventure buddies, she can be found running, trying to teach her cat tricks, or relaxing with friends at a brewery.

Advocate with your...

WORDS

It's easy to get overwhelmed and confused by where to start in advocating to end the stigma surrounding mental health. However, you can start right now, with your words.

PRONOUNS: It may sound cliché, but you never know who you could be helping by identifying your pronouns. Pronoun labels vary: she/hers, him/his, them/theirs among many other terms. Those who use pronouns that may differ from their physical appearance, or the sex that they are assigned at birth, are often ostracized. This, in turn, can feel isolating and lead to exacerbation of a diagnosis that may already exist (like generalized anxiety or depression) or could lead to the beginning of one.

The step of identifying pronouns starts with you saying yours! The next time you run a meeting or are meeting someone new, saying your pronouns may help them feel comfortable sharing theirs.

STOP USING DIAGNOSTIC WORDS IN EVERYDAY LANGUAGE: I am sure most of us have done it: referring to a behavior or quality in someone as "OCD" or "bipolar," among other diagnostic labels. It may seem harmless, but using these phrases is very stigmatizing and brings negative connotations. It is also belittling to those who do live with these diagnoses every day.
Instead, try talking about the qualities of the behavior or action, without the label.

"DEATH BY SUICIDE" VS "COMMIT SUICIDE"

This change in terminology is crucial. When we talk about someone "committing suicide," it insinuates that a crime was committed (i.e., someone *commits* a murder) as opposed to dying from an illness like cancer. Changing the terminology reflects the important fact that those who die by suicide do so because of mental illness.

ACTIONS

Got the language down? Awesome! Let's talk about your actions. You can start by identifying yourself as an "ally" or "safe person" to those who live with mental illness, and by getting to know the resources in your community.

Looking to get even more involved? Consider volunteering and answering phones at a crisis hotline. Or start a fundraiser for an advocacy or research organization!

Part 5

Words from Our Allies

Kathy's Brownies

Ingredients:

- 4 squares (4oz.) unsweetened chocolate
- 1 cup unsalted butter
- 2 cups sugar
- 4 eggs
- 1 tsp. vanilla
- 1 cup flour
- a dash of salt

Notes to add my own voice to this recipe!

Directions

1. Preheat the oven to 350F degrees.

2. Melt the chocolate and butter in a large bowl.

3. Beat in the sugar. eggs. and vanilla until they are fully mixed.

4. Add the flour and salt. but just incorporate. You do not want to overmix the batter.

5. Grease a 13x9-inch pan well. or lay down foil in the pan and grease the foil. so that you can lift the brownies out of the pan.

6. Bake the brownies for 20-25 minutes.

7. Cool. flip over. and cut into desired sizes.

8. Enjoy! They are amazing with vanilla ice cream.

Author's Note:

In creating this chapter of the book, I wanted to give space to commemorate the words and actions of those who helped me work through my "darkest hour," and who, in turn, have seen me develop into the advocate and person I am today.

Kathy Threadgold was my first introduction to hope in a very dark time. She has made me (and continues to make me) a better person, and she says that I have made her a better therapist. Our work together means more to me than she will ever know. Even though we do not work together consistently anymore, she always seems to know what to say. The Christmas of the year we met, I was watching It's a Wonderful Life with my dad, when he said to me, "Kathy is your Clarence." Even now, when we write to each other, we sign off as TO/FROM Clarence and George, like the guardian angel and hero in the movie. She will always be my guardian angel and has so much wisdom to share. The piece below always gets me though the most difficult moments. She has held on tight with me through this journey, and has taught me that challenges bring lessons with them, even when you can't see them in the moment. I never seem to be able to see them right away, but Kathy always does.

Ally Note:

"Despair takes us in when we have nowhere else to go...grief is a temporary home for self-reflection. It lets us heal and move on from a place of emptiness to one of self-love and compassion. It only stays long enough to teach us what we need to learn. Trust the process. Not having an answer keeps us paying attention and looking within."

BIO

Kathy Threadgold

Kathy Threadgold is a Metro West Massachusetts-based therapist. She has held many roles in the clinical and human services professions before creating a private practice out of her home. She works with people of all ages and backgrounds. Kathy has a loving family and enjoys spending time with those who mean the most to her. She loves the beach, and is a big proponent of mindfulness meditation and trusting the process.

Julia & Lea's Cookie-Brownie

Ingredients:

- 8 Tbsp. unsalted butter, room temperature
- ½ cup white sugar
- ¼ cup brown sugar
- 1 egg
- ½ tsp. vanilla
- 1 cup + 2 Tbsp. flour
- ½ tsp. baking soda
- ½ tsp. salt
- 1 cup chocolate chips
- Your favorite brownie mix and all ingredients called for on brownie mix box

Notes to add my own voice to this recipe!

Directions

1. Preheat the oven to 350F degrees.

2. Cream the butter and sugars in a medium mixing bowl. Add the egg and vanilla, and cream again until smooth. Next, stir in the flour, baking soda, and salt with a wooden spoon until fully combined. Add the chocolate chips. Set aside in the refrigerator until ready to use.

3. Prepare the brownie batter as directed on the box. Pour the batter into an 8x8-inch or 9x9-inch baking dish. Scatter the pieces of cookie dough randomly over the top of the brownie batter.

4. Bake for 35-40 minutes (or 30 minutes for gooey brownies, 35-40 minutes for a glass dish). Remove from the oven and cool for at least 10 minutes. Cut into 16 bite-sized pieces.

Author's Note: In creating this chapter of the book, I wanted to give space to commemorate the words and actions of those who helped me work through my "darkest hour," and who, in turn, have seen me develop into the advocate and person I am today.

The two women here share not just this page but also their love of writing. Lea Sullivan was my sixth-grade English teacher, and we keep in contact to this day, 15 years later.
I met Julia Guilardi when I was a senior in college and she was a freshman. I took Julia under my wing first, within a student organization, but she has since taken me under her wing in life. I am so grateful to have both women supporting me and cheering me on. I love to do the same for them, as they are both extremely talented in so many ways.

Julia shares this recipe and why it is her go-to:

"This is my go-to recipe to bring to family gatherings and parties with friends. Because of this, it always reminds me of how much love I have in my life and how grateful I am to have such a strong support system! It also represents how I love to celebrate those who are most important to me."

Lea shares her wisdom to compliment the cookie-brownie:

"The most important ingredient in life is being comfortable in your own skin. I wish I knew that earlier on, but I am grateful for the ways I have learned the lesson. My mantra during any challenge is "put one foot in front of the other."

BIO

Julia Guilardi

Julia Guilardi is a graduating senior at Northeastern University, majoring in journalism with minors in law and linguistics. Born and raised just outside of Philadelphia, she currently lives in Boston, where she has to pretend she cares about professional sports. After graduation, she'll be working as an editor at BookBub, an e-book marketing startup in Cambridge, MA. In her free time, she loves to read, bake, and watch Arrested Development reruns on Netflix (but only up to season three). She is philosophically opposed to the Oxford Comma.

Lea Sullivan

Lea Sullivan has been very fortunate to teach in the town of Southborough, MA, for a lifetime. She loved teaching English to fantastic middle school students (like the author, Dayna), who taught her as much as she taught them. After retiring, Southborough allowed her to transition into "real" retirement by reinventing herself annually in different roles for ten years. She loves being with her family, playing with her grandchildren, traveling, and gardening.

Andy's Mocha Cake

Ingredients:

Cake
- 1 cup unsalted butter, softened
- 3 cups brown sugar, packed
- 4 eggs
- 3 tsp. vanilla extract
- 3 cups all-purpose flour
- ¾ cup baking cocoa
- 3 tsp. baking soda
- ½ tsp. salt
- 1½ cups brewed coffee, cooled
- 1 & 1/3 cups sour cream

Frosting
- 12 oz. cream cheese, softened
- 6 Tbsp. unsalted butter, softened
- 6 oz. unsweetened chocolate, melted
- 6 Tbsp. brewed coffee
- 2 tsp. vanilla extract
- 4½-5½ cups powdered sugar

Notes to add my own voice to this recipe!

Directions

Cake

1. Preheat the oven to 350F degrees.

2. In a large bowl. cream the butter and brown sugar until light and fluffy.

3. Add the eggs. one at a time. beating well after each addition. Beat in the vanilla.

4. Combine the flour. cocoa. baking soda. and salt. Add to the creamed mixture alternating with the coffee and sour cream. beating well after each addition.

5. Pour into three greased and floured 9-inch round baking pans. Bake for 30-35 minutes. or until a toothpick inserted near the center comes out clean.

6. Cool for 10 minutes before removing from the pans to wire racks. to cool completely.

Frosting

1. In a large bowl. beat the cream cheese and butter until fluffy.

2. Beat in the chocolate. coffee. and vanilla until blended.

3. Gradually beat in the powdered sugar. Spread the frosting between the layers and over the top and sides of the cake.

4. Cover and refrigerate until serving.

Author's Note: In creating this chapter of the book, I wanted to give space to commemorate the words and actions of those who helped me work through my "darkest hour," and who, in turn, have seen me develop into the advocate and person I am today.

I cannot think of anyone more fitting for this chapter than my dad, Andy Altman. Although he has always been my dad, we really became close when I began my mental health journey. He truly went above and beyond to understand the process with me. My dad has always been my role model. A lifelong and humble leader, he is the "calm rock" in the ocean of Altman anxiety. But he is more than that - he is our foundation, and I am excited to share here with you the wisdom that he shares with me!

Ally Note:

All who know me know that I am certainly not one who bakes or cooks. I do, however, make a great soup for my kids when they are not feeling well, but for that, I only need a can opener.

There are certain food items, though, that I truly obsess over. One of these is the underappreciated mocha cake. What could be better than combining coffee and chocolate? Although the only effort I expend is in finding the best bakery that I can, I do find meaning in this incredible dessert.

To me, when having this dessert, I am always thinking about how worthwhile the extra effort was to get my favorite mocha cake. The bakery is far away and there is never a good place to park. So much easier to just settle for a less meaningful, but easier to obtain, dessert. But the easier dessert is not as good! It is always important to reward yourself for a job well done, or to reward yourself for nothing in particular. You are your own best friend and should always go the extra mile for yourself.

BIO

Andy Altman

Andy Altman is the very proud father of the author. Dayna. and her sister. Jamie. As he nears 60 years old. he has realized quite clearly that this is his greatest achievement. and he is so lucky to celebrate this on a daily basis with his loving and talented wife. Sheryl.

He is constantly striving to improve his golf game. his fantasy football team. and his many Spotify playlists. After selling his business. he now runs the Rodman Division of Brown & Brown Insurance. and greatly hopes that this new role in no way takes away from the time he loves to spend in always-sunny Florida.

Liah & Caroline's Cake Pops

Ingredients:

- Chocolate or vanilla cake (prepared): can use box directions to prepare

- 1 full container chocolate frosting or vanilla frosting

- 2 bags (24oz.) chocolate chips

- Cake pop sticks

- 1 container sprinkles

Notes to add my own voice to this recipe!

Directions

1. Put the prepared cake in a large bowl.

2. Crumble the cake until it resembles fine crumbs.

3. Add in the frosting, two tablespoons at a time, to moisten the cake until it can hold a ball shape. You can use your hands to do this.

4. Use a mini ice cream scoop to scoop out the cake mixture. Use whichever scoop size you prefer.

5. Roll the mixture until it forms a tight ball, then put it on a plate. Repeat until all the cake mixture has been rolled into balls.

6. Melt 2-4 ounces of chocolate chips in the microwave.

7. Dip the tips of the cake pop sticks into the melted chocolate and insert into the cake balls about halfway.

8. Freeze for 20 minutes, and in the meantime, prepare the decorating supplies.

9. Melt the remaining chocolate in a large cup. Make sure you have enough chocolate to completely submerge the cake ball.

10. Remove the cake balls from the freezer.

11. Dip each cake ball carefully into the chocolate until covered. Let the excess chocolate drip off.

12. Add the sprinkles while the chocolate is still wet - it will harden quickly.

13. Stick the decorated cake pop into a Styrofoam block to finish setting.

Author's Note: In creating this chapter of the book, I wanted to give space to commemorate the words and actions of those who helped me work through my "darkest hour," and who, in turn,
have seen me develop into the advocate and person I am today.

Liah Malley
This book would not be complete without making space for my friend, Liah, so I created below a list of things I learned from her!
The 10 Things Learned from Liah Malley (on and off the bike)

No matter how bad you feel, talking to Liah Malley might just turn your whole day around. One of the kindest and most genuine people I have ever met, Liah is a Boston-based Soul-Cycle (indoor cycling company) instructor, yogi, Lululemon Ambassador, adventure enthusiast, and mom to her newborn, Summit Rose, and dog, Ellie. She is an all-around lover of life, among many other things.

Taking Liah's classes at SoulCycle and being Liah's friend, I have learned so much, but here are the top 10:

1) **Don't try to push away the discomfort (on or off your bike): lean in and learn how to live in it. That is where you grow.**

2) **Tell people how you feel! Own how you feel and share it!**

3) **Love is the greatest tool: if you let it lead you, you are unstoppable.**

4) **Don't hold back in anticipation of what is coming next. If you do, you might miss it.**

5) **When you let go of the people who try to bring you down, when you give the negative words less power, you become more authentic.**

6) *There is nothing wrong with being yourself. The world will love you for it.*

7) *Show up for the people around you - it is always worth the time.*

8) *The last eight are the best eight (in SoulCycle context,this would be after a set of difficult arm choreography during the arm strength training portion of class, but outside of class I take this to mean the following): the last part is the best part - ride it out and wait to see what is on the other side.*

9) *There is nothing wrong with a bad day - people will still love you for you.*

10) *Making people feel special, feel good, feel appreciated, seen, and heard is the best thing we can do for each other...so show up for each other - it is all we've got!*

Caroline Geehan

Similarly, my friend Caroline Geehan inspired the piece below. She has also been an integral part of my healing, and has taught me the following:

I have always found the best kind of friends are those you can go weeks or months without talking to, and then pick up as if nothing has changed. Of course, I would love to talk to Caroline every day (if you knew her, you would too!), but as we grow older, our lives get busier, days seem to get shorter, and friendship dynamics can change.

Although the amount of physical time I have spent with Caroline over the years has changed, I could not be more grateful that we have become so close.

I met Caroline when I started my fourth year of college and had an internship at Boston Children's Hospital, where Caroline worked. We have both grown in different ways and are at different points in our lives, but we see each other through life's challenges just the same. Caroline was one of the first people I opened up to about being sexually assaulted, and she welcomed my story with open arms. She showed me so much love and support, to the point where I began to feel comfortable speaking up about my experience and moving forward in my life as a survivor.

When I met Caroline, she had recently received a small plate (to hold jewelry) with the saying "The best is yet to be." When she showed this to me, the saying became our code. In the toughest moment or when things feel too hard, we remind each other "The best is yet to be." I believe both this sentiment and my friendship with Caroline really get at the heart of resilience. This is not to say that we should disregard the present moment, as it brings its own beauty, but there is something about this saying that inspires holding on to the tiniest bit of hope. This is a reminder that when things feel too hard, there is always something brighter on the horizon. The best is yet to be.

Notes, Thoughts & Goals

Jan & Kim's Yodel Cake

Ingredients:

- 2 boxes yodels

- 2 gallons favorite ice cream
  (Mocha Chip ice cream pictured)

Notes to add my own voice to this recipe!

Directions

1. Take the ice cream out of the freezer to soften.

2. Slice all of the yodels horizontally.

3. In a large bowl, place the sliced yodels in a line (with the end pieces facing out).

4. Put the softened ice cream on top of the yodels.

5. Fill the whole bowl with ice cream.

6. Cover and freeze.

7. Turn the bowl over a plate. You can use a warm sponge and run it over bowl to help ease the cake onto the plate.

Author's Note: In creating this chapter of the book, I wanted to give space to commemorate the words and actions of those who helped me work through my "darkest hour," and who, in turn, have seen me develop into the advocate and person I am today.

Both Jan and Kim Feinberg (mother and daughter), my great-aunt and cousin, have important lessons to share here. Jan ("Gunky," as we call her in my family) and I have had the opportunity to make time to have lunches together once a month. I love being able to spend this time with her, learn from and be loved by her.

Kim is my outgoing cousin who has kept me laughing for the last 26 years. I appreciate her not only as a cousin but as a friend!

Ally Note:

Jan
I would encourage anyone reading this to count their blessings. It is so important to be grateful for what you have. It can really bring perspective and, in turn, can help you live life to the fullest. "Life is not a dress rehearsal."

Learned from an Ally: Kim

Kim Feinberg, my dear friend and cousin, local Boston celeb-dog walker, does not give herself enough credit! When I asked her for her best advice if a friend was going through a difficult moment, I think I caught her off guard. But what she doesn't know is that just being herself is sometimes the best thing for someone having a hard time. Kim is hilarious, always has a story to tell, and is so loving in her approach. You might not know it, but you may be a "Kim" to someone. So if you are unsure how to help a friend or family member who is struggling, just be you. Sometimes a little bit of love, a lot of laughs, and a good story may help the people in your life more than you think.

BIO

Jan Feinberg

Janice Feinberg is a 75-year-old woman who recently retired from her long-time job at Macy's. Since retiring, she has completed many items on her bucket list. In fact, she has never been busier. She is often heard saying "how did I work?" Between knitting, crocheting, cooking, and spending time with her loved ones, she is enjoying every moment of life.

Abulini's* Flan submitted by Sophia Romeu

Ingredients:

- 5 eggs
- 1 can (14oz.) condensed milk
- 14 oz. milk (recommend whole or 2%)
- 5 Tbsp. sugar
- water

"This dessert recipe is a family favorite. I have fond memories of my Abulini* visiting us when I was a child. Abulini usually arrived late in the afternoon or at night, and one of the first things we would do together is make flan. This was perfect because my family loves to eat flan all times of the day, especially for breakfast...Yes, with this recipe you can have dessert for breakfast too!

*Abulini is my family's affectionate name for my grandmother, who is from Buenos Aires, Argentina." -Sophia Romeu

Notes to add my own voice to this recipe!

Directions

1. Preheat the oven to 350F degrees.

2. Place the sugar in the baking pan mold, and melt it on the stovetop until golden caramel in color. Let it cool. *Soph Tip: Move the mold around to swirl the melted sugar so that it coats the bottom of the tin. This will help ensure that the sugar does not burn, and that an even melt is created.*

3. Crack the eggs into the mixing bowl, and add both the condensed milk and cow's milk. *Soph Tip: Keep the empty can of condensed milk and use this as a measuring cup - fewer dishes to do at the end.*

4. Pour the mixture into the mold with the caramel sugar. You will most likely hear crackling. Don't worry, crackling is a good sign - it means that your sugar set perfectly.

5. Place the mold into a baking pan. It is important to make sure this pan has sides because next you will fill the base pan with an inch of water.

   (Soph Note: My Abulini calls this a "a baño Maria." You do this to make sure that your flan cooks with a little steam, which keeps it moist and supple.)

6. Put both pans in the oven for one hour.

7. Allow time for the mold to cool (about 15 minutes), then wrap the mold or cover with a plate to chill for at least eight hours in the fridge. Soph Tip: Allowing the flan to chill overnight makes the wait time much easier. Plus, you can even sleep in a bit longer since a protein-rich breakfast will be ready when you wake up.

Directions

8. Using a plastic or wooden knife (you don't want to scratch the pan), lightly outline the flan - both the inside and outside edges. Soak the pan in a bit of warm water to loosen the caramel and make for a clean flip. Then take your desired serving plate and place it on top, right in the center of the pan. Then flip, serve, and enjoy!

Author's Note: In creating this chapter of the book, I wanted to give space to commemorate the words and actions of those who helped me work through my "darkest hour," and who, in turn, have seen me develop into the advocate and person I am today.

Sophia and I became friends right at the start of my mental health journey in 2010, when I was introduced to treatment, diagnoses, medication - new everything. When I asked her to contribute to the book, she created the beautiful poem below, and I am grateful to commemorate it here.

Ally Note:

hymn for the...

...mind

i have only one and she is precious
she is strong, but i am stronger
she seems to have a constant source of energy, but i can choose to be still while she run circles around me
she is full of thoughts, memories, feelings, but i choose what to love and what to let go of
but remember, i have only one, she is precious... she is me.

...spirit

i have only one and she is precious
she grows in a garden filled with sunshine, rich soil and a pot-pourri of plants and flowers with the river of life running through her
she is easy to neglect and needs tending
sometimes taking care of her can feel like a chore, but it's not, it's a practice of self-love
but remember, i have only one, she is precious... she's me.

...heart

i have only one and she is precious
she may not be the first thing you see - she gets stage-fright
at times - but i promise you she's always there
there are even times when she becomes so full that her juices
begin to leak from my eyes
this is how she cares of me; this is how she sets herself free.
but remember, i have only one, she is precious... she's me.

BIO

Sophia Romeu

Sophia Romeu has been friends with the author, Dayna, since they met in college in 2010. Sophia works as the Social Media and Digital Content Coordinator at Jacob's Pillow. She absolutely loves classical music, sparkling water, and playing with every dog she meets. You can often find Sophia searching for the next culinary experience, spending time with her family and friends, and hiking in her favorite place, "the Berkshires," in Western Massachusetts.

ACKNOWLEDGEMENTS

To thank everyone who has been involved in supporting this book would truly be impossible, but I will do my best.

Thank you Jason Sondu Taglieri for designing and publishing this book. I am so appreciative of your willingness to change and edit the book through each cycle. It has been an honor to work with someone so dedicated and passionate.

Thank you, Charlotte Breslin from Skeleton Key Editing for professionally editing this book.

Thank you Brenna Stewart of Brenna Stewart of Photography for taking the photos for this book. You have been with me from the beginning and I could not be more grateful to be on this journey with you, so special to work with you.

Thank you Dena Tranen for writing such a meaningful Forword and believing in me every step of the way. You always tell me you will be with me "as long as it takes", you prove it every time.

Thank you Kristen Pompey (KP Phuntography), and Christina Spleen (Christina Anne Photography) for taking the supplemental photos for this book, it means so much!

Thank you to Eve Altman for doing the initial proofreading - you never let anything go unnoticed!

Thank you to all who contributed to this book. Without your willingness to be vulnerable, this book would not exist.

Final thanks to my support system for never doubting my ability to complete and CONQUER a project.

PHOTO CREDITS

Christina Anne Photography: pgs. 3, 27
Brenna Stewart Photography: pgs. 9, 41, 55, 65, 71, 77, 83, 91, 97, 109, 119, 123, 129, 143, 147, 161, 165, 171, 177, 187, 193, 197, 203, 209, 239, 243, Front & Back Cover
KP PHUNTOGRAPHY: pgs. 15, 35, 47, 115, 183, 221, 225, 229, 233
Suzanne Garveich: pg. 21
Kara Lyon Photography: pg. 135
Andrea Foley: pg. 151
Marie Louise: pg. 155
Dayna Altman: 213

About the Author

Dayna Altman is an enthusiastic and driven young professional based in Boston MA. She currently works as the Substance Use Prevention Program Coordinator at Girls Inc. of Lynn by day and is an entrepreneur in her spare time. Her entrepreneurial adventures have helped her become a speaker, a documentary film maker and now a published author.

Notes, Thoughts & Goals

Notes, Thoughts & Goals

Notes, Thoughts & Goals

Notes, Thoughts & Goals

CPSIA information can be obtained
at www.ICGtesting.com
Printed in the USA
BVHW060049040320
573615BV00001B/1